LAURIE SHIFRIN

Batik Gems

29 Dazzling Quilt Projects

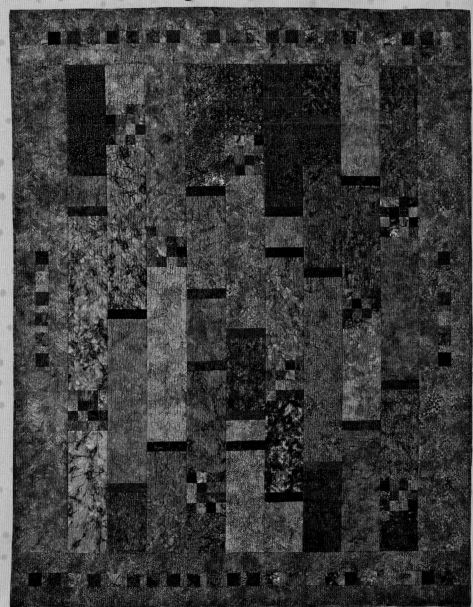

C&T PUBLISHING

Text copyright © 2008 by Laurie Shifrin

Artwork copyright © 2008 by C&T Publishing, Inc., and Laurie Shifrin

Publisher: Amy Marson

Creative Director: Gailen Runge

Acquisitions Editor: Jan Grigsby

Editors: Susan Beck and Kesel Wilson

Technical Editors: Carolyn Aune and Robyn Gronning

Copyeditor/Proofreader: Wordfirm Inc.

Cover & Book Designer: Christina D. Jarumay

Production Coordinator: Casey Dukes

Illustrator: Tim Manibusan

Photography by Luke Mulks and Diane Pedersen of C&T Publishing unless otherwise noted

Published by C&T Publishing, Inc., P.O. Box 1456, Lafayette, CA 94549

Library of Congress Cataloging-in-Publication Data

Shifrin, Laurie J.

  Batik gems : 29 dazzling quilt projects / Laurie Shifrin.
    p. cm.
  Summary: "Make 29 vibrant batik quilts in colors that span the rainbow and in sizes from crib to king size."—Provided by publisher.

  ISBN 978-1-57120-560-5 (paper trade : alk. paper)

  1. Patchwork—Patterns. 2. Quilting—Patterns. 3. Appliqué—Patterns. 4. Batik. I. Title.

  TT835.S4657 2008
  746.46'041—dc22
                                    2008013100

Printed in China

10 9 8 7 6 5 4 3 2

DEDICATION

I dedicate this book to the memory of my mother, Rosalyn Shifrin. She instilled in me a love for fabric and introduced me to the art of creation. As I grew older, this developed into my passion for designing and making quilts. Although she never made a quilt herself, she did outfit four daughters and numerous Barbies. I'll never forget the look of awe on her face the time I showed her my first quilt, which I'd made while away at college.

ACKNOWLEDGMENTS

My life in Seattle has been greatly enriched by my good friends Janine Jijina, Deb Brooks, Caroline Thompson, Suanne Rakel, Joan Johnstone, and Diane Roubal. All are former colleagues from the In The Beginning quilt store and have become wonderful friends. They have encouraged and supported me through all the stages of creating quilts for this book. Thank you one and all.

A special thanks to my good friend and professional long-arm quilter Carrie Peterson, whose creative ability and dedication helped make the quilts even more special.

Thank you to my binding fairies—Barbara Rincon, Judy Schleis, Karen Chesnut, Marlene Bissell, and Jo Moen (truly the binding queen)—who helped bind many of these quilts.

My gratitude goes to my Quilt Market buddies: Anne Moscicki, Amy Butler, and Diane Capaci. You helped give me the confidence that what I create is worth sharing with the rest of the quilting world. Thanks for the boost!

Having the support of the many fabric companies that produce batiks constantly renews my love for their gorgeous fabrics. Thanks to the following:

* Island Batik
* Timeless Treasures
* Hoffman California-International Fabrics
* Princess Mirah Design/Bali Fabrics
* Bold Over Batiks!
* Lunn Fabrics

Thank you, Quilters Dream Batting, for producing and providing me with my favorite cotton batting.

Dr. Joyce Mori's books, *Native American Designs for Quilting* and *Quilting Patterns from Native American Designs* (American Quilter's Society, 1998 and 1993) inspired some of the quilting designs used on my quilts. I have used Dr. Mori's books for years and consider them a great source for unusual quilting designs.

Inspiration comes from many sources. I found it in the work of ceramic artist Orla Kaminska (www.orlakaminska.com), who created the gorgeous clay tile seen on page 81, and Bonnie Wilkins (www.bonniewilkins.com), who designed the unique note card on page 33. Thank you both for allowing me to print these images and for awakening creativity in my quilt designs.

I feel privileged to be working with the wonderful staff of C&T Publishing, who are committed to producing gorgeous and inspirational quilt books.

FOREWORD

Almost weekly I get asked, "When is your next book coming out?" followed by "What's the topic?" I have honestly never considered doing anything other than more batik quilts. It's rare in life when something calls to you with a force as strong as I feel for creating quilts using batik fabrics. Even more rare is the opportunity to turn that passion into a career.

I have been lucky twice in my life, first with music, in which I had a satisfying career as a professional violinist. That career enabled me to enrich people's lives while traveling around the United States and Italy. Now, once again, I am fortunate to feel drawn to another creative art and to be able to turn it into a career. Through lecturing and teaching, I have the opportunity to inspire others while traveling around our amazing country, seeing landscapes and wildlife that continue to inspire me.

Another source of my inspiration came from attending a lecture and slide show by Valori Wells in which she showed many of her photographs of patterns found in nature. I felt a kinship with her, and she challenged me to look more closely at every plant and flower I encountered. The purchase of my first digital camera changed my life, and now I'm never without it.

Living in the Pacific Northwest provides me with an ever changing landscape of superb mountain ranges and wondrous vistas overlooking huge bodies of water. With nature as my constant inspiration, I have designed quilt patterns that I hope will be an inspiration for you.

Contents

Introduction

Inspiration and creativity are the two driving forces behind my quilting. I love designing interesting patterns and exploring new color combinations. For this book, I've designed ten new patterns, each very different from the others. In addition to showing each pattern in two fabric combinations, I've included instructions for making most of the quilts in multiple sizes, so that from this book alone you could make at least 29 different quilts. Thus, you have many options for the overall size and look of your quilt. In addition to the project instructions, I've also given you a glimpse into what inspires me to be creative, whether it's a scene in nature, a gift card, or a ceramic piece.

Each of the ten patterns consists of easy patchwork pieces that can be rotary cut, and all the quilts are fairly easy to make. With basic quilting skills, you'll be able to make any of the projects in this book. The simplest patchwork patterns are found in *All Tucked In*, page 25; *Crossroads*, page 73; and *Vertical Vision*, page 20. Even *Phinney Ridge*, page 40, and *The Queen Charlottes*, page 47, which look complicated, are easy to piece. *Coral Fantasy*, page 64, is nothing but a traditional star block repeated in a variety of value combinations. *Coming Full Circle*, page 87, is basically composed of Log Cabin blocks; and *Bits & Bars*, page 80, is made completely of squares and rectangles.

Two of the patterns, *Falling Ginkgo Leaves*, page 32, and *Broken Garden Path*, page 56, include simple appliqué. I've given you my favorite appliqué techniques for each of these, but feel free to use whatever technique you are most comfortable with.

The quilts all feature a wide variety of batiks, and two quilts showcase gorgeous Asian prints as the main fabrics. Although my love of batiks is limitless, I realize that batiks don't appeal to everyone (though I can't imagine why!). I hope that you'll use my patterns to make the quilts using the type of fabrics you love most, and if you've never used batiks, give them a try. Batiks are so easy to work with, and they create lush, warm-looking quilts.

Most of the quilts in this book can be considered scrappy. Don't be intimidated by the prospect of making a scrappy quilt—I'll guide you through the process, and I have included a whole section titled Successful Scrappy Quilts, pages 10–15. I've also included tips throughout, including suggestions for making some of the quilts appear less scrappy by using fewer fabrics.

I've tried to show quilts in every color group I could imagine, although if I were making the quilts just for me, they would all be in some unusual shade of green. (I think living in Seattle, where the ever present rain keeps things lush and green year-round, has influenced my color choices.) I encourage you to look beyond my samples and explore the quilt patterns in new color combinations.

To aid you in your fabric selection and quilt assembly, I've included useful tips throughout the book that can be applied to these projects as well as your future projects. I hope you'll enjoy giving the tips a try and making the ones you like part of your quilting life.

Bali Batiks

Batiks have invaded the quilting world, and they keep getting more and more gorgeous. These hand-made fabrics created for quilters are crafted almost exclusively on the Indonesian island of Bali (a few are made in India). Highly skilled artisans create colors, designs, and textures that sparkle like jewels and inspire quilters worldwide.

Batik is a wax-resist method of decorating fabric. The base fabric is generally poplin, broadcloth, or cambric, which all have smooth, fine fibers in a tight weave. The tight weave offers clarity in the design that a looser weave wouldn't allow. Most often, the base fabric is dyed an initial color or blend of colors that will end up as the color of the motif or design in the final product.

Heavy copper tsaps are used for stamping wax on fabric.

The stamped fabric is dipped in or painted with dye, usually a darker color than the first. The waxed portions resist absorption of the dye, retaining the first color. The fabric is then set to dry in the sun. This waxing process can be repeated multiple times with the same design or a different design that appears as subsequent colors.

After the initial dyeing, the design is stamped across the entire surface of the fabric with a heavy copper tsap (pronounced "chop") and melted wax, which is a combination of beeswax and paraffin. The tsaps are 4–14 inches in size and take months to make.

Examples of designs from multiple tsaps or tsaps in multiple colors

The dried fabric is immersed in boiling water, which causes the wax to float to the surface. The wax is skimmed from the water, and the fabric is removed and set out to dry again. In the places where the wax was applied, the design appears in the first applied color.

During the dyeing process, the fabric can be dipped multiple times to achieve more depth of color. The dye can also be applied using many different techniques, some involving chemical reactions. A fabric can go through a dozen or more steps before it is a finished product.

There are many, many variations on this procedure, and each creates a unique effect. The above steps produce a design motif that is lighter than the background.

Design motif is lighter than background.

In the next sample, you'll notice that the design motif is darker than the background. To achieve this effect, the fabric goes through extra processes. The first few steps are the same: the base fabric is dyed overall, this time in a darker color or colors. The wax is applied, and then the fabric is essentially bleached to take the unwaxed portion back to the base color, or as close to it as possible. Next, the fabric is immersed in the overall background color, dried, and boiled to reveal the darker design.

Design motif is darker than background.

There is an entire category of fabrics that are not batiks but are meant to be used in combination with batiks. These are hand-dyed fabrics to which no wax was applied. The manufacturers of these fabrics have their own names for them: technique dyes, handpaints, hand-dyes, solids, and so on. Each company's artists develop new techniques to achieve exciting and distinct effects.

Here are some of the many varied textures available in dyed fabrics. Every time I look, there are new textures—the designers must know that quilters always want something new!

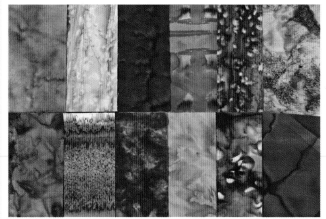

Examples of hand-dyed, non-batik fabrics

For more information on the making of and history of batiks, the Internet is a wonderful resource. For hands-on experience in making batiks, many local quilt shops and art supply stores offer classes.

unique qualities of batiks and hand-dyed fabrics

Owing to the various processes done by hand to each piece of fabric, no square foot of fabric is exactly like any other square foot. Part of the beauty of working with handmade fabrics as opposed to machine-manufactured fabrics is that you feel a sense of the artisans actually stamping, painting, and boiling the fabrics, as well as a sense of the culture that produces those artisans. For me, using batiks is like cooking with meat and produce obtained from local farmers—you know what the animals were fed and what went into the soil.

In batiks, you will find many characteristics that may seem like imperfections but are merely the nature of handmade goods. I prefer to think of these imperfections as rustic qualities and choose to celebrate their uniqueness.

One common irregularity arises during the stamping. If the tsap was not exactly aligned with the previous stamping, you may see the designs overlap. This irregularity is most obvious in linear or small, repeated patterns.

If tsap isn't perfectly aligned on successive stampings, designs will overlap slightly. Handmade goods often have such "imperfections."

Although most batiks are completely reversible, occasionally you'll find a batik on which the wax hadn't fully penetrated to the back side, making the design less clear on that side. Usually, you have to look hard to find the discrepancy, in which case don't worry about right and wrong sides; but in obvious cases, choose the clear, distinct side as the right side. Choosing the right side becomes important primarily for large border pieces. You wouldn't want to have three sides with distinct designs and one side with fuzzy designs.

Wrong side

Right side

Wrong side

Right side

Wrong side

Right side

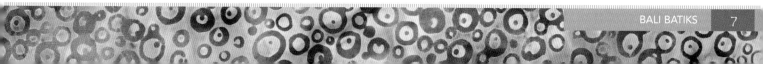

Sometimes the colors will be more vibrant on one side of batiks and hand-dyed fabrics. I choose the richest, brightest side, unless the duller side better suits my project.

Dull side   Bright side

Dull side   Bright side

Once you have chosen the fabrics for your project, check to see whether they have right and wrong sides. That way you'll be aware of which fabrics need special attention.

handling and care of batiks, hand-dyed fabrics, and other quilting cottons

Batiks and hand-dyes have many unique qualities but can be treated like, and used in combination with, any other quilting cotton. I recommend prewashing all your cotton fabrics. You can prewash when you purchase your fabrics, as I do, or just before you use them. There are many reasons for prewashing:

✿ You may find little speckles or small clumps of *wax residue* left on your batiks. It looks ash-colored or even yellowish. You can fleck some of it off with your finger-nail, but don't try to iron it out—it will melt into the fabric and discolor it. The wax will come out in the wash.

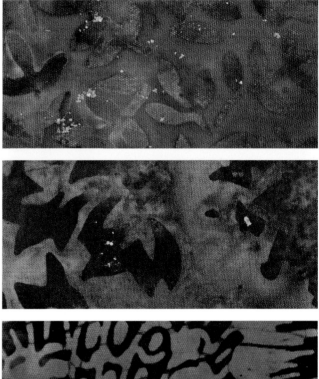

Remove wax residue by washing (not ironing) fabric.

✿ Many dark-colored hand-dyed fabrics may *release their color*—or bleed—in the wash.

✿ Non-batiks often have a *chemical finish* on them that helps prevent fading. Some people have an allergic reaction to the finish, and you should certainly wash the finish from any fabric that may come in contact with infants.

✿ Because batiks have been wetted, dried, and boiled multiple times and because the fibers are fine and the weave is tight, batiks will not shrink. However, most non-batiks *will* shrink in the dryer (sometimes over 3″ from selvage to selvage), and you want that shrinkage to happen *before* you add these fabrics to your quilt.

selvages

We all know that you shouldn't use the selvage of quilting cottons in your quilts. Almost all regular cottons (non-batiks) have selvages, which often have labeling, pinholes from the printing machines, and irregular shrinkage. When you look at the selvages on batiks and hand-dyes, you'll see that there isn't any labeling and there are no pinholes; the fibers are basically consistent all the way to the edge except for the final, larger thread on the very edge. Therefore, you may think that you don't need to trim anything off the edge. However, I recommend trimming $\frac{1}{4}$"–$\frac{3}{8}$" to make sure you don't use the very edge, which is often slightly wavy.

Occasionally you'll find that the stamped design doesn't go all the way to the edge of a batik fabric, and all you see on the edge is the background. In those cases, it's best to trim the portion that doesn't have the design.

Trim portion of edge that doesn't contain design.

washing and drying instructions

Wash your fabrics in groups of similar values (darks, lights). Use a gentle, phosphate-free soap, such as Orvis or Quilt Wash, *cold* water, and a gentle or short cycle. If you use anything but cold water, you are inviting release of the dye, or bleeding, which may result in loss of the vibrancy of the colors.

It's a good idea to check for bleeding by scooping some rinse water into a white cup so you can see whether it's running clear. If you see color in the rinse water, then your fabric is releasing its dyes. In most cases, one or two extra cold rinses will wash out any excess dye. If you have a real problem bleeder, that is, you still see color in the rinse water after multiple cold rinses, you can try adding white vinegar to the next rinse, although this may have limited effectiveness. Or you can add Synthropol to the rinse water, following the manufacturer's directions. Synthropol is a chemical, sold at quilt shops, that removes excess dye from the fabric and prevents the dye in the water from settling on other fabrics. If you have sensitive skin, wear rubber gloves when using Synthropol, and make sure you wipe up any spills.

To dry your fabrics, remove the pieces from the washing machine and untwist and untangle them if necessary. Don't overload your dryer (dry only 4–5 yards per load) and dry on *hot* until the fabric is thoroughly dry. Remove the fabrics immediately and press following the tips to the right.

pressing tips

One of the amazing qualities of batiks is that they hold a crease extremely well without the use of steam. Most other quilting cottons press almost as well; therefore, I recommend *not* using steam when you press, *especially* when working with batiks. If you do use steam, be aware that the steam, in combination with the weight of the iron, will often distort the fabric as you are ironing.

Exception: If the fabric is very wrinkled when it comes out of the dryer, steam may help you press the wrinkles out. Press *parallel* to the selvage, along the less stretchy lengthwise grain, and you'll have a straighter selvage edge than if you iron perpendicular to the selvage.

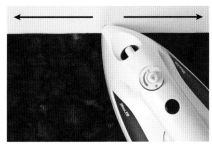

If you must use steam, press *parallel* to selvage along lengthwise grain.

If you have a fabric that doesn't want to hold a crease, such as an Asian print with gold metallic accents, you may need to use steam. Be careful not to distort the piece.

Be aware that we all tend to over-press and that each piece gets pressed many times during the construction of a quilt top. Your main goal in pressing during the piecing process should be to orient the seam allowances in the desired direction.

Successful Scrappy Quilts

When you think "scrappy," you may think of a quilt with lots of small pieces of dozens and dozens of different fabrics—like a postage stamp quilt. To me, scrappy means that the same fabric doesn't appear in the same place over and over. There is a feeling of randomness to the placement, which lends flow to the quilt.

Scrappiness can apply to just one part of the quilt while other parts stay consistent throughout. In *Phinney Ridge*, page 40, the yellow bars are scrappy (they're made from seven fabrics), as are the small squares next to the large border rectangles. The rest of the quilt has specific fabrics designated for each part.

Coming Full Circle, page 87, is scrappy in the sense that each of the circles is made of a different fabric, but the parts that form that circle are all of one fabric.

The Queen Charlottes, page 47, and *All Tucked In*, page 25, are scrappy in that you need a bunch of fabrics, and those fabrics intermingle throughout the parts of the entire center of the quilt.

Falling Ginkgo Leaves, page 32, can be considered scrappy because the background is made up of seven fabrics that can be switched around at will.

Using a variety of fabrics in your quilts makes them more visually interesting. To me, a successful quilt is one in which fabrics appear to interact in different ways each time you look at it. When I was a violinist in a professional orchestra, I played the same piece of music, such as Beethoven's Fifth Symphony, dozens of times. At each performance I would hear some new balance of instruments or an inner counterpoint instead of just the main melody, and that's what kept it interesting. That's the true test of whether a work of art will have longevity.

The same applies to quilts. If there is a feeling of motion, instead of stagnation, throughout the quilt, you are more likely to discover new relationships between the fabrics.

Instead of being an object that is fixed and lifeless, the quilt can be an organic work of creativity.

Read on to learn more about selecting and arranging fabrics to create your beautiful quilts.

selecting your fabric

Choosing fabrics is the most creative part of making a quilt, and it can also be the greatest challenge. We want assurance that our finished quilt is going to be pretty and worth the effort and the expense. Many people purchase kits because they know how the finished quilt will look and that it'll be a sure success (if they like the sample).

I encourage you to be brave and choose your own fabrics. There really isn't a right or wrong fabric selection, but there are lessons to be learned from each quilt. Try moving out of your comfort zone as far as colors are concerned; venture into new color groups. For instance, if you always lean toward bright colors, try subtle, earthy fabrics.

If you take a little guidance from the following sections, I can steer you toward a more pleasing fabric arrangement, but no matter which fabrics you choose, make the quilt and try to learn from the experience. Do what I do—say to yourself, "Next time, I would eliminate…" or "I would have liked more…" or "That fabric didn't work because…"

JEWEL TONES AND EARTH TONES

Almost all batiks can be placed into one of two color categories: jewel tones and earth tones. The fabrics used in *Vertical Vision*, page 20, are good examples of full-saturation jewel tones. Rich purples, magentas, sapphires, and emeralds make up the majority of colors used here. The second quilt from that pattern, *Into the Woods*, page 21, is an example of the exact opposite, earthy colors reminiscent of moss, leaves, and the rich bounty found outdoors.

Jewel tone fabrics

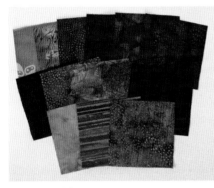
Earth tone fabrics

A common mistake my students make is to combine the two color categories and end up getting a mixed-identity quilt. This can happen when quilters move into a color range they aren't comfortable with—like bright jewel tones—and then try to tone the fabrics down by putting in a few earth tones. Or sometimes quilters select all earth tones and feel that the quilt needs some zip, so they add a few jewel tones, which then seem out of place. In either case, the resulting quilt lacks a cohesive feeling because the quilter didn't commit to one palette.

ADDING LIGHTS

The traditional approach to fabric selection is to choose a range of light, medium, and dark fabrics to achieve contrast. *That's an approach I never take!* Contrast can be achieved by a using a variety of colors, or by mixing patterns with solids.

If you flip through this book, you'll notice that most of the quilts are of medium value, without a lot of value contrast, as in *Bits & Bars*, page 80. Even *The Queen Charlottes*, page 47, doesn't have any truly dark fabrics, and I eliminated the really light fabrics.

An exception is *Phinney Ridge*, page 40, in which the seven yellows contrast strongly with the dark teals and dark olives. Notice, however, that the light fabrics aren't really all that light and that they have a warmth that complements the other fabrics.

Light fabrics in the two color categories, earth tones and jewel tones, often tend to be either too gray-looking or sweet pastel. Neither look enhances the medium and dark fabrics. In fact, I find that the lights often water down the effect of the rich, darker batiks. Below are examples of cool pastels and gray earthy solids. Instead of these, look for rich medium lights that you might not have initially considered as lights.

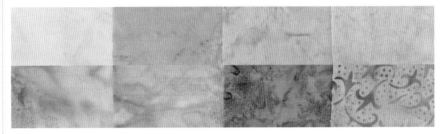
Poor choices (top) versus better choices (bottom)

Another option is to choose light fabrics that have small prints in darker values or are multicolored to tie them in to the rest of the fabrics.

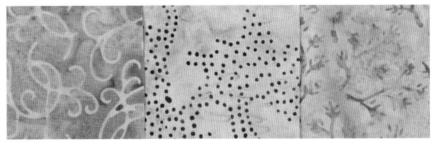
Light fabrics with small or dark-value prints make good contrast fabrics.

The fabric on the far left is a plain and somewhat boring yellow; the three fabrics to the right are more-interesting choices for lights or contrast fabrics.

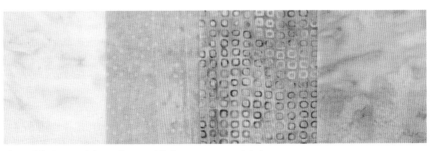
Three fabrics on right make good lights or contrast fabrics.

Avoid fabrics that "glow in the dark" in relation to the overall mix. These are fabrics that are distracting in their lightness. In *Summer Celebration*, page 65, I wanted a light green for the sashing to make the colors of the stars pop, but I had to try about six different fabrics before I found one that didn't read as neon.

Avoid "glow in the dark" fabrics. Audition as many fabrics as it takes to find the right one, as I did with the above sashing.

THE GLANCE TEST

My favorite technique for testing whether a fabric should stay in or come out is my *glance test*. Step back a few feet and look away from your group of fabrics. Take a quick glance back (for about a second) and ask yourself "Which fabric catches my eye first?" If it's that glow-in-the-dark, light fabric, chances are that that fabric is all you're going to see when you look at the finished quilt. If the eye-catching fabric is the one and only truly dark fabric, try adding another dark fabric to draw your focus away from the lone dark.

If, when you glance at your group of fabrics, you see that you have too many fabrics of one color and not enough of others, you can either add more of the others or choose to use proportionately less of each of the similar fabrics. That way, you get to keep the variety without overwhelming the quilt.

When all is said and done, if you are unsure whether a fabric should stay in, go ahead and cut the necessary pieces. You'll have the choice of whether to use them or not later in the process.

HALFWAY POINT

A good practice for making scrappy quilts is to make half of the total required blocks, using some of each fabric. Place the blocks on your design wall and give them the *glance test*. If one fabric catches your eye, decide whether the standout fabric is a good distraction, providing pop and sparkle, or a bad distraction, preventing you from seeing the quilt as a whole. Determine whether the fabric adds to the quilt or detracts; you should keep only the *positive contributors*.

If you want your quilt to be primarily a blue quilt, but the green is overpowering the blue, then use fewer green pieces in the remaining blocks and consider adding more blue fabrics. If you like the yellow, but there's just too much of it, make the rest of the blocks without the yellow and distribute the blocks containing yellow around the entire finished quilt. If the big, garish print that you weren't sure about still stands out too much, remove blocks containing it and make replacements. Or if you just feel you need more variety, choose some additional fabrics. In the remaining blocks, incorporate the new fabrics with the old.

The halfway point is your chance to be sure you like your fabric selection.

FABRIC SELECTION TIPS

Your main fabric selection goal for a quilt should be to aim for a *cohesive color palette* with a variety of textures: each of the fabrics feels comfortable in the mix, and nothing leaves you feeling unsettled. Use the following tips to help ensure that you'll be pleased with your final fabric selections.

❋ Choose a *theme fabric* or border fabric with colors and a print that you love. Choose the rest of the fabrics so they don't compete or overpower this main fabric. Use the colors from the main fabric to guide you as you select the rest of the fabrics.

❋ Beware of *flat, textureless* batiks that read as solids. They can be showstoppers—but not in a good way! Always opt for a batik that has some texture or a small print.

Flat solids (top) versus textured solids (bottom)

✳ A batik with white or very *light spots* or printing on it, like the examples below, will catch the eye, especially if there is only one such fabric. It may add sparkle, or it may be distracting. You decide.

Batiks with white or very light spots can be good or bad, depending on your other fabric choices.

✳ Using many solid, one-color hand-dyes is the safe choice. Mixing *multicolored hand-dyes* and small- to large-scale prints with those solids makes a much more interesting quilt. You may run into a batik that has a *large-scale print* that you don't care for, but colors that you love. Remember that when the fabric is cut into relatively small pieces (which is likely), it might make a great mixer.

Even multicolored or large-scale prints can work well when small pieces are used.

✳ *Striped batiks* are great! They're versatile and make great inner borders and bindings. A big striped piece might stand out a little, as in *The Queen Charlottes*, page 47. In this case, it is a little distracting but not detrimentally so.

Striped batiks are versatile and can add visual interest to your work.

✳ If you have a multicolored, mottled fabric with big splotches and *not all the colors work* in your quilt, you can fussy cut away the parts that don't go with your project.

✳ If one of your fabrics stands out as an *oddball* (there are no others like it, and you're not sure it works), but you really want to include it, just add one or two others like it so it won't stand out quite so much.

✳ In scrappy quilts, it's always *better to have too many fabrics* than too few. If you have too few, your eye will look for nonexistent patterns in the placement of each fabric. So, when I say "eight or more" or "four or more," I really mean get as many as you can afford. The more the merrier. That way, individual fabrics won't stand out, and the colors will blend to become more homogenous. The quilt will appear to have a random look, making you see the overall effect instead of individual fabrics.

✻ Try to **stretch the color palette** instead of matching all the fabrics. Monotone is boring, so if, for instance, you're making a quilt of mostly blues, use some fabrics that are green-blue and some that are red-blue and some that are pure blue.

✻ One of the greatest misconceptions I run into is the notion that there's no such thing as an ugly batik, that if you don't like a fabric, you must not "get it." **Not every batik is a pretty batik**—there *are* some duds. You're allowed to be as discriminating as you are with non-batiks, and not every fabric will find a place in one of your quilts. (Leave the duds for other people who may just love them.)

✻ Accept that if you're buying fabrics for your stash, you may not use them for quite some time. I do feel that batiks, more than other printed quilting cottons, tend to be timeless and not just trendy. Still, what you thought was pretty five years ago may not be what you're into this year. So **accept some failures** without regret—and donate to friends!

arranging a scrappy quilt

Your design wall is your most useful tool for arranging the parts of your scrappy quilt. Place the blocks and other parts in the appropriate arrangement, referring to the quilt assembly diagrams found with each project. Choose blocks randomly at first, paying little attention to fabric distribution; then follow these guidelines for getting a well-balanced quilt.

✻ Identical or similar fabrics should be distributed throughout the quilt. Similar fabrics may be ones of the same color or the same scale of print.

✻ Decide which are the most outstanding fabrics—the darkest, lightest, brightest, or busiest. You can find these by using the *glance test* described on page 12. Another way to decide is to look at a spot right next to the quilt and use your peripheral vision to catch fabrics that stand out. Make sure to distribute these fabrics throughout the quilt.

✻ If there is an oddball fabric (a busy print when the rest are subtle, or a bright orange in a sea of blue), distribute pieces of the fabric around the quilt in an asymmetrical fashion (that is, don't put pieces in the same row or same column).

✻ If you selected a fabric you weren't sure you were going to like in your quilt, and you still don't like it even after you have the blocks made—*take it out!* Making a few more blocks and being happy is always better than regretting the use of a fabric you don't like.

✻ If there are fabrics that have a warmer feeling, make sure they appear in all areas of the quilt.

✻ Be sure that all the pieces of one color aren't grouped in one area, unless that's your artistic intent.

✻ Aim for a look of **planned randomness**. The arrangement should look random, but you should have had to work a little to achieve that look. If the fabrics have relationships to one another, random secondary patterns will sometimes emerge.

✻ Lastly, the goal is a well-balanced look. Acknowledge that there is no *one* right arrangement; you could re-arrange forever and never find the perfect setup. Find an arrangement that is pleasing and then call it a night. The next morning, take a quick glance at it with a fresh eye.

Once you are pleased with the arrangement, take a digital photo. The digital image can help you spot distractions in the layout that the naked eye can't see. If nothing stands out as uncomfortable or wrong, call it good!

a lesson in flexibility

Even with the best planning, you may occasionally find that after the center of your quilt top is assembled, the border fabric you've selected doesn't quite complement the quilt, perhaps because the border isn't dark or weighty enough to frame the center or because the border needs to be subtler to showcase the center. Or perhaps you just don't love the border fabric enough for a quilt that has turned out to be so stellar!

Whatever the reason, allow yourself to be flexible. Flexibility is actually a good thing during all stages of making a quilt. Rigid determination to use a fabric just because you've paid for it may lead to quilts that don't live up to their full potential. And flexibility is key to the learning process. Follow your instincts.

I made the alternate version of *The Queen Charlottes*, page 47, using three different border fabrics. The border on *The Sprinkler's On!* was the inspiration for all the fabrics used in the blocks, but when I put the blocks on my design wall, I became unsure about the border fabric; it seemed too busy or too light, so I went to my stash and found two other choices.

I had made enough blocks and side triangle units for the Twin size, but I decided to split them up to make three small quilts. I divided the colors up almost equally, but I used more of the lightest fabrics with the lightest border, and the darkest fabrics with the darkest border.

I ended up with three beautiful quilts and thought it would be fun to show you how different a quilt can look depending on what frames it. When all is said and done, I prefer the original light and busy border because the quilt reminds me of droplets of water scattered by a sprinkler through my dad's summer garden. It makes me want to jump under the spray of water!

The Sprinkler's On! II

The Sprinkler's On!

The Sprinkler's On! III

Tips and Techniques

As an educator, I like to offer tips for making my students' quilting lives a little easier, and to pass along useful hints that I've figured out in almost 30 years of quilting. In the following sections, you'll find helpful advice for using this book, as well as some of my favorite techniques for general assembly and for finishing your quilt. I hope you'll read through these sections and give my tips a try.

about the instructions

As we all know, every author has her own style of writing directions. The following list gives insight into my approach to writing directions and will help answer some of the typical questions that might arise when you start a new project.

◎ Read through the directions for the entire quilt before you begin cutting.

◎ Yardage requirements for each quilt include enough fabric for shrinkage, for straightening the cut edge, and in most cases, for one error in cutting the largest-size piece, so unless you tend to make multiple cutting errors or your fabric measures less than 40" widthwise after shrinkage, the recommended yardage should be plenty.

◎ I have listed measurements for batting that is 3" larger than the quilt top on all sides and backing that is 4" larger on all sides (after

shrinkage). The extra inches will make it easier to lay out your quilt sandwich without much fuss. Or, if you send your quilt to a longarm quilter, you will meet his or her requirements.

◎ All the binding yardages are for straight-grain binding. If you prefer bias binding, add 1/8–1/4 yard of fabric and cut your strips on the bias.

◎ All cuts are widthwise—from selvage to selvage—unless otherwise stated.

◎ On charts for multiple sizes, I recommend using a highlighter to mark the column for the size you are making. Marking will help you keep track of the number of pieces you are cutting and what size they should be. Use a different color if you make a different size next time.

◎ Make the size that fits your needs. For example, if you have a queen-size bed but want a lot of overhang and some extra fabric to tuck under the pillow, make a king-size quilt or consider altering the border widths to achieve your desired size.

◎ Cut more pieces than you'll need of each scrappy element. That way, as you assemble the quilt, you'll have the choice to use more of the fabrics you like and less of those that aren't working as well. Cutting extra elements gives you the flexibility to get the best combination of colors—you won't be restricted by a limited number of pieces.

◎ Before you begin sewing any of the projects, I recommend that you test your seam allowance and stitch length. Cut three 2" squares of the type of fabrics you will be sewing (batiks or regular quilting cottons). Using a small stitch length (10–11 stitches per inch, or a stitch length of 2.5mm), sew these squares into a chain. Press the unit and measure its length. If it's not 5" long, then you may need to adjust your seam allowance. When I teach, I have everyone use a *slightly* scant 1/4" seam allowance, by which I mean about two threads of fabric less than a full 1/4". This adjustment makes up for what you lose in pressing.

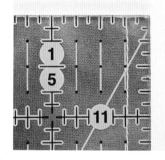

◎ Press after *each* and *every* step. Pressing will increase your accuracy and ensure that your finished quilts are smooth and flat.

◎ I have not provided basic sewing directions or instructions for layering, basting, or quilting your quilt. If you need help with these techniques, refer to *The Art of Classic Quiltmaking* by Harriet Hargrave and Sharyn Craig, which is available from C&T Publishing, or one of the many other general quilting books available.

tools

There are products out there that can make your quilting life easier. The following are a few tools I can't live without when working with batiks or making scrappy quilts:

◎ **Schmetz Microtex Sharp machine needles, size 10**: These are slender, sharp needles to be used with tightly woven, high-thread-count fabrics. You'll hardly notice them going into the fabric, whereas other types of needles seem to *thunk, thunk* through the fabric.

◎ **Fresh rotary cutter blade**: Treat yourself to a fresh blade! You'll be amazed at how much less effort it takes to cut your fabrics. If you are comfortable with rotary cutting equipment and haven't tried the 60mm cutter, think about upgrading. The larger the blade, the less the work.

◎ **Fine, sharp glass-head pins (1¼"–1⅜" long; 0.50 or 0.60mm steel shaft)**: Because batiks are tightly woven, you want pins that slip through the fibers easily without leaving a big hole when removed. The glass heads are baked on and will not pull off like plastic heads, and the glass heads are smaller so the pins will lay flatter against the machine bed. I prefer Collins brand number C103.

◎ **Design wall**: Are you one of those people who put their blocks on the floor or on a bed to arrange them? Find a place to hang a design wall (even if it's over closet doors), and you'll be able to get a much better view of your blocks. You need to be able to step a few feet away (ideally 5–10 feet) to get a good perspective. My favorite product is Quilt Wall 72" Square.

helpful tips

Here are a few of my favorite tips to help you achieve more accurate piecing. You'll find many more tips throughout the book.

HANDLING TRIANGLES

When handling cut pieces—especially triangles—hold them with one hand. If you use two hands, you may stretch the bias edges. When I teach, I frequently say, "Don't overhandle the pieces."

Wrong way to handle cut pieces: with two hands

Right way to handle cut pieces: with one hand

CHAIN STITCHING

When chain stitching, it's important to keep your eye on the pair of pieces that you are sewing; see the pair through *to the end* before you pick up the next pair. If you start thinking about the next pair before you finish the first, the seam allowance tends to vary, especially when you are sewing triangles. Also, leave ¼"–⅜" of thread between pairs instead of butting them one against the other. Then, when you cut them apart, the stitches will not immediately begin to come undone.

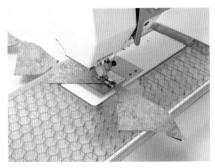

When chain stitching, focus on the pieces you are sewing, not the next set.

STRAIGHT GRAIN VS. BIAS GRAIN

If you are sewing a straight-grain piece to one with a bias edge, stitch with the straight-grain piece on top whenever possible. The presser foot tends to stretch the top piece, so having the naturally stretchy piece on top wouldn't be good. Likewise, if one piece is shorter than the other, stitch with the shorter piece on top. The presser foot may help stretch the top piece, and the feed dogs will help ease the bottom, longer piece.

COMBINING BATIKS WITH REGULAR QUILTING COTTONS

As you have read, batiks are made on a fine-fibered, tightly woven fabric. This means there will be little or no stretch as you are working with them. That is not the case with almost all other quilting cottons. The fibers are fatter and more loosely woven, which leads to … stretching. So, whenever possible, place the non-stretchy piece (the batik) on top and the stretchy piece (the non-batik) on the bottom for piecing.

adding borders

Many of the quilts in this book have borders pieced from multiple fabrics. Directions are provided with those quilts. *Use the following instructions for quilts with borders made of one long piece and for which I have not specified the exact border length in the cutting directions.*

If there are inner and outer borders, follow Steps 1–6 for the inner borders first; then repeat the steps for the outer borders.

1. For side borders, measure the quilt top through the center of the quilt, from top edge to bottom edge. On a large quilt, this is sometimes awkward to do, and the easiest way may be to fold the quilt in half and lay it flat on your cutting table to measure.

2. Divide the total measurement in half to get the midpoint. For example, if the quilt measures $62\frac{1}{2}$", the midpoint is $31\frac{1}{4}$". Mark the midpoints of the sides of the quilt with pins.

3. Fold each of your long side-border pieces in half the long way (short ends together) and mark the center point with a pin. From the center point, measure the distance you determined in Step 2. For example, in the above case, measure $31\frac{1}{4}$" from the center of each border piece. Place a pin securely in each layer at the measured point. That is where the edge of the quilt *should* hit. You now have three pins in each side border piece.

4. *Don't cut* the borders to the new measurement. With the borders on top, pin a border to each side of the quilt, starting at the center point, leaving the marking pins in place. Place pins every 4"–6", distributing any fabric that needs to be eased in. Remember that the machine will assist with the easing; the presser foot will stretch the top piece, and the feed dogs will help ease in the underside.

If both border pieces are too small (as often happens) and there is too much extra fabric to ease in (more than $\frac{3}{4}$" or so), it's OK to add up to $\frac{1}{2}$" *total* to both side borders (not just one side, or the quilt won't be symmetrical). I usually add the smallest amount I can to make the easing work better. This is why you shouldn't cut the borders to length before you have a chance to adjust them.

5. With the border pieces on top, sew them to the quilt. Press the seams toward the borders. Trim both ends of each side border even with the quilt top.

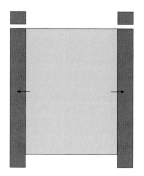

6. Measure the width of the quilt top through the center, including the borders you just added. Follow Steps 2–5 to attach the top and bottom borders.

a few words about machine quilting thread

There are so many thread options for the final creative stage in making your quilt—the quilting. For machine quilting, whether you choose to do it yourself or have a professional longarm quilter do the work, thread selection is an important decision. Batiks have a variety of colors, shades, and textures across the length of the fabric—there is nothing flat about batiks. If you want the quilting to complement the fabric as opposed to standing out from the fabric, try choosing a variegated thread with similar variations in color or value so the quilting will blend with the majority of the colors and values of the fabric. That way, you'll see the quilting designs flow in and out, just like the colors of the fabric.

Detail of *Vertical Vision*, page 20

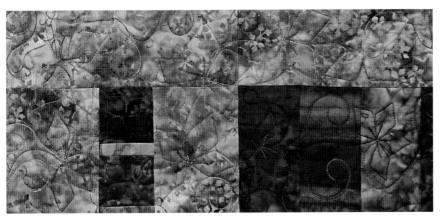

Detail of *Bits & Bars*, page 80

Detail of *All Tucked In*, page 25

Choose variegated thread that doesn't have too great a value change within one spool; if a thread goes from really light to really dark, the extreme portions of the thread will usually show too much on the fabric. Instead, look for color variation within one value—all lights to medium lights, or all mediums to medium darks.

Some of my favorite variegated cotton threads are shown here. They include King Tut from Superior Threads, YLI variegated cotton machine quilting thread, Sulky Blendables (use the 30 weight to blend or the 12 weight to make a statement), and Valdani hand-dyed variegated thread. There are many other choices, and I encourage you to look for the colors that best suit your project instead of sticking to just one brand.

a bit about batting

I like to use cotton batting in all my batik quilts. Cotton gives a flat, even appearance, which is perfect for a wallhanging. Cotton batting also clings to the fabric, which gives a drapey look that I love for a lap or bed quilt. Polyester batting, in contrast, often tends to give the look that the pieced quilt top is floating over the batting and not connecting with the batting or backing.

My favorite cotton battings are the two lightest weights from Quilters Dream Batting, Request and Select (see Resources, page 95, for contact information). They are great for both hand and machine quilting. Many brands of cotton batting are available, and you should give a few of them a try to come up with your favorite.

finished quilt sizes

LAP/TWIN, 52½" × 64½"
DOUBLE/QUEEN, 70½" × 88½"
KING, 88½" × 112½"

On a trip to a local nursery, I was intrigued by the scouring rush, shown here with its tall stalks of green and black.

This photo became the inspiration for two quilt patterns in this book. In *Vertical Vision,* it translated into straight vertical bars interrupted at irregular intervals by dark thin rectangles. The sixteen-patches break up the vertical bars even further, adding visual interest. I have a huge stash of every shade of purple, and I knew they would be perfect for this quilt. Even though I stayed in one color family in each of the two samples, you should feel free to explore multiple color combinations.

Have you ever gone to buy batiks, fallen in love with a gorgeous colorway, and had the choice of multiple prints in that colorway? The borders of this quilt provide a great opportunity to use four prints in one color. You *can* also use just one border fabric, as I did in *Into the Woods.* If you are using four border fabrics, wait to cut them until the center of the quilt is pieced. Then, working on a design wall, decide which fabric looks best on which side of the quilt.

You can reduce the number of fabrics by using only one contrasting fabric for the narrow rectangles that divide the columns, as I did in *Into the Woods.*

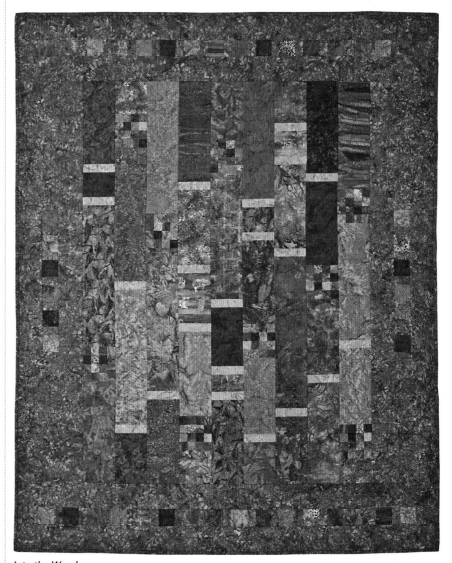

Into the Woods
Lap/Twin, 52½" × 64½"
Designed, pieced, and quilted by Laurie Shifrin.

fabric requirements

Fabric	Lap/Twin (52½" × 64½")	Double/Queen (70½" × 88½")	King (88½" × 112½")
8 or more medium pink/purple fabrics	½ yard each	¾ yard each	1¼ yards each
Dark contrast fabrics			
if using 3–4 fabrics	¼ yard each	⅓ yard each	⅜ yard each
if using 1 fabric	½ yard	⅝ yard	⅞ yard
Coordinating border fabrics			
if using 4 fabrics	½ yard each	¾ yard each	⅞ yard each
if using 1 fabric	1⅞ yards	2⅜ yards	2⅞ yards
Binding	¾ yard	⅞ yard	1 yard
Backing	3⅝ yards	5⅝ yards	8½ yards
Batting	59" × 71"	77" × 95"	95" × 119"

cutting instructions

	Lap/Twin (52½" × 64½")	Double/Queen (70½" × 88½")	King (88½" × 112½")
NOTE: The number in parentheses is the quantity to cut. Pieces are cut in order of size, largest to smallest.			
From medium pink/purple fabrics			
Strips*	2 strips each, 4½" × fabric width; minimum of 12 strips	2 or 3 strips each, 6½" × fabric width; minimum of 20 strips	3 or 4 strips each, 8½" × fabric width; minimum of 25 strips
*Total number of strips given allows for 2 extra strips so you will have choices.			
From above strips (Label each piece with its letter to avoid confusion when assembling the quilt top.)			
D	(1), 4½" × 18½"	(1), 6½" × 27½"	(1), 8½" × 36½"
E	(2), 4½" × 17½"	(2), 6½" × 26"	(2), 8½" × 34½"
F	(3), 4½" × 16½"	(3), 6½" × 24½"	(3), 8½" × 32½"
G	(1), 4½" × 15½"	(1), 6½" × 23"	(1), 8½" × 30½"
H	(2), 4½" × 14½"	(2), 6½" × 21½"	(2), 8½" × 28½"
I	(1), 4½" × 13½"	(1), 6½" × 20"	(1), 8½" × 26½"
J	(3), 4½" × 12½"	(3), 6½" × 18½"	(3), 8½" × 24½"
K	(1), 4½" × 11½"	(1), 6½" × 17"	(1), 8½" × 22½"
L	(7), 4½" × 10½"	(7), 6½" × 15½"	(7), 8½" × 20½"
M	(4), 4½" × 9½"	(4), 6½" × 14"	(4), 8½" × 18½"
N	(1), 4½" × 8½"	(1), 6½" × 12½"	(1), 8½" × 16½"
O	(2), 4½" × 7½"	(2), 6½" × 11"	(2), 8½" × 14½"
P	(2), 4½" × 6½"	(2), 6½" × 9½"	(2), 8½" × 12½"
Q	(2), 4½" × 5½"	(2), 6½" × 8"	(2), 8½" × 10½"
R	(2), 4½" × 4½"	(2), 6½" × 6½"	(2), 8½" × 8½"
S	(4), 4½" × 3½"	(4), 6½" × 5"	(4), 8½" × 6½"
T	(1), 4½" × 2½"	(1), 6½" × 3½"	(1), 8½" × 4½"
From remainder of medium pink/purple fabrics			
B**	(30 total), 2½" × 2½"	(40 total), 2½" × 2½"	(170 total), 2½" × 2½"
A	(130 total), 1½" × 1½"	(130 total), 2" × 2"	(A and B are the same size)

From 3–4 dark contrast fabrics			
B**	(20 total), 2½" × 2½"	(24 total), 2½" × 2½"	(62 total), 2½" × 2½"
A**	(32 total), 1½" × 1½"	(32 total), 2" × 2"	(A and B are the same size)
C	(21 total), 4½" × 1½"	(21 total), 6½" × 2"	(21 total), 8½" × 2½"

****For border squares B, choose fabrics that will show against your border fabric(s). Low contrast is fine, but the squares shouldn't totally blend in and become invisible. Also, I have you cut extra squares for the sixteen-patch blocks and for the pieced border so you'll have choices when you are piecing them.*

From each of 2 of the 4 coordinating fabrics for side borders ***			
W	(2), 8½" × 16"	(2), 8½" × 28"	(2), 8½" × 40"
V	(2), 3½" × 17½"	(2), 3½" × 17½"	(2), 3½" × 17½"
U	(5), 1½" × 2½"	(5), 1½" × 2½"	(5), 1½" × 2½"

From each of the 2 remaining fabrics for top and bottom borders ***			
Y	(2), 3" × 2½"	(2), 3" × 2½"	(2), 3" × 2½"
X	(15), 1½" × 2½"	(15), 1½" × 2½"	(27), 1½" × 2½"
Z	(3), 3½" × fabric width Piece strips together end-to end. Trim to make 2 strips 3½" × 52½".	(4), 3½" × fabric width Piece strips together end-to end. Trim to make 2 strips 3½" × 70½".	(5), 3½" × fabric width Piece strips together end-to-end. Trim to make 2 strips 3½" × 88½".

***If you're using only 1 border fabric, cut all the above border pieces, cutting the largest pieces first.

From binding fabric			
Binding	(7), 2½" × fabric width	(9), 2½" × fabric width	(11), 2½" × fabric width

---

cutting tip

Label each piece with its letter to avoid confusion when assembling the quilt top.

quilt assembly

For all 3 sizes:

Use a ¼" seam allowance. Press the seams in the direction of the arrows.

1. To make sixteen-patch blocks, randomly select 4 different small squares A. Stitch the squares together to form a strip. Press the seams in one direction. Repeat to make 36 strips.

fabric tip

Decide which fabrics are the most outstanding (lightest, darkest, brightest) and make sure a few of these appear in each sixteen-patch.

2. Select 4 of the strips and arrange them so the seams head in alternate directions. Stitch the 4 strips together to make a sixteen-patch. Press the seams in one direction. Make 9 sixteen-patch blocks.

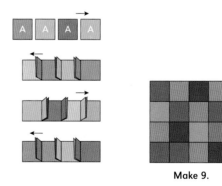

Make 9.

stitching tip

To make it easier to select adjacent strips with the seam allowances going in opposite directions, lay the strips on a table, wrong sides up.

3. Referring to the quilt assembly diagram, right, arrange the sixteen-patch blocks, rectangles C, and pieces D–T on the design wall. Pieces of the same size can be interchanged to get the best possible arrangement— well balanced with evenly distributed colors and values. Pieces within a vertical column can be shifted within that column if doing so makes a better arrangement.

4. Once you are pleased with the arrangement, stitch the pieces of the vertical columns together. Press the seams away from the sixteen-patch blocks and rectangles C. Stitch the columns together. Press the seams away from the center.

border assembly

Directions are given for using 4 different border fabrics.

SIDE BORDERS
For all sizes:

1. Using pieces cut from the left border fabric, select 6 border squares B and the 5 side border rectangles U. Sew the pieces into 1 long strip, alternating the squares and rectangles. Press the seams in one direction.

Sew segments to form strip.

2. Sew a rectangle V to each long side of the strip. Press. Add a rectangle W to each end. Press.

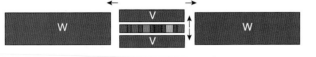

Add rectangles V; add rectangles W.

3. Repeat Steps 1 and 2 for the right side border using pieces cut from the other side-border fabric.

TOP AND BOTTOM BORDERS
The top and bottom borders vary for each quilt size. Pieces are referred to by letter name. The Lap/Twin size appears first, with the amounts for Double/Queen and King sizes in parentheses.

1. Using pieces cut from the top border fabric, select 16 (22, 28) border squares B, 15 (21, 27) rectangles X, and 2 rectangles Y. Stitch the pieces together to form 1 long strip. Press the seams in one direction.

Assembly of top and bottom border squares

2. Sew a large rectangle Z to each long side of the strip. Press.

Top and bottom borders

3. Repeat Step 1 using the bottom border pieces.

4. Sew the side borders to the sides of the quilt. Press. Sew the top and bottom borders to the quilt. Press.

5. Layer, baste, and quilt as desired. Bind and add a label.

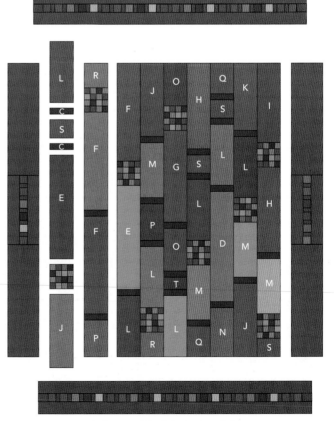

Quilt assembly diagram for all sizes

All Tucked In

Double, 65½" × 85½"

Designed and pieced by Laurie Shifrin. Quilted by Carrie Peterson.

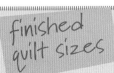
finished quilt sizes

Lap/Twin, 55½" × 65½"
Double, 65½" × 85½"
Queen/King, 89½" × 99½"
Finished Block Size: 7"

Simple quilts can be beautiful, as is the case with *All Tucked In*. It doesn't get much simpler—large plain blocks, quarter-square triangle blocks, and easy pieced blocks—but what a fun result! Put all the pieces together and you have an intriguing and complex quilt. Whether you need to make a quick lap quilt or you want a new king-size quilt for your bedroom, this pattern is a snap.

This pattern looks great in any grouping of fabrics—retro prints, Asian prints, delicate florals, country golds and blues, and, of course, batiks. Go wild and mix small and large prints, multicolored fabrics and tonals or mottled fabrics, and if you've never made a quilt set on point, this would be a great place for a first-time effort.

Note that in *All Tucked In*, the small setting triangles are of an unobtrusive fabric that is different but similar to the border fabric. In *Midnight Blues*, I used the border fabric itself for the setting triangles. A contrasting fabric would also work and would give definition to the center of the quilt. For the thin inner borders, I chose subtle, undulating fabrics, but a high-contrast fabric would have an entirely different effect. There really are unlimited possibilities!

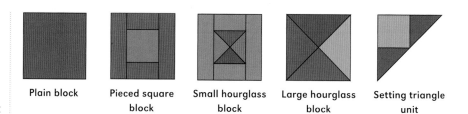

| Plain block | Pieced square block | Small hourglass block | Large hourglass block | Setting triangle unit |

This stunning quilt is made from very simple blocks: plain blocks, pieced square blocks, small hourglass blocks, large hourglass blocks, and setting triangle units.

Midnight Blues
Lap/Twin, 55½" × 65½"
Designed and pieced by Laurie Shifrin.
Quilted by Carrie Peterson.

fabric requirements

Fabric	Lap/Twin (55½" × 65½")	Double (65½" × 85½")	Queen/King (89½" × 99½")
10 or more assorted fabrics for blocks	⅜ yard each	⅔ yard each	⅞ yard each
Side and corner setting triangles	⅝ yard	⅝ yard	¾ yard
Inner border	¼ yard	⅓ yard	⅜ yard
Outer border	1¾ yards	2¼ yards	2¾ yards
Binding	⅔ yard	¾ yard	⅞ yard
Backing	3¾ yards	5½ yards	8½ yards
Batting	62" × 72"	72" × 92"	96" × 106"

cutting instructions

For	Cut	Lap/Twin (55½" × 65½")	Double (65½" × 85½")	Queen/King (89½" × 99½")
From 10 or more assorted fabrics for blocks				
E	8¼" × 8¼", then ⊠	6 total □ to make 24 △	15 total □ to make 60 △	30 total □ to make 120 △
F	7½" × 7½"	14 total	20 total	26 total
D	4¾" × 4¾", then ⊠	6 total □ to make 24 △	12 total □ to make 48 △	21 total □ to make 84 △
C	4" × 4"	20 total	32 total	47 total
B	2¼" × 7½"✳	24 total	48 total	84 total
A	2¼" × 4"✳	24 total	48 total	84 total

✳You need 2 matching As and Bs for each block.

For	Cut	Lap/Twin (55½" × 65½")	Double (65½" × 85½")	Queen/King (89½" × 99½")
From fabric for setting triangles				
G	6¼" × fabric width	2	2	3
	Crosscut strips into 6¼" × 6¼", then ⊠	7 □ to make 28 △	10 □ to make 40 △	13 □ to make 52 △
H	Cut remaining 6¼" strips into 5⅞" × 5⅞", then ◺	2 □ to make 4 ◥	2 □ to make 4 ◥	2 □ to make 4 ◥
From inner border fabric				
Inner border	1" × fabric width	5	7	8
From outer border fabric (lengthwise cuts)				
Outer border	For Lap/Twin and Double, cut strips 7½" × fabric length	4	4	—
Outer border	For Queen/King, cut strips 9½" × fabric length	—	—	4
From binding fabric				
Binding	2½" × fabric width	7	8	10

◩ = cut square diagonally to make half-square triangles
⊠ = cut square twice diagonally to make quarter-square triangles
□ = squares
◸ = half-square triangles
△ = quarter-square triangles

The following diagrams are suggested layouts for cutting the different parts from the block fabrics; the diagrams assume you are using 10 fabrics. It's nice to have extra pieces for the blocks when making scrappy quilts, so you can use this same layout if you have more fabrics.

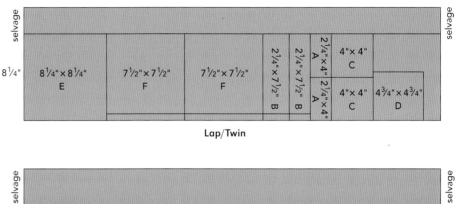

Lap/Twin

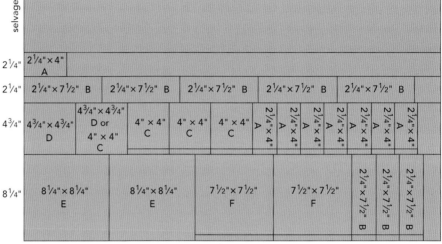

Double

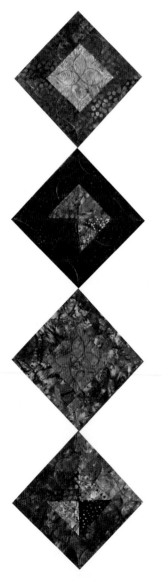

Queen/King

quilt assembly

Use a ¼" seam allowance. Press the seams in the direction of the arrows.

Refer to the block chart below for the required number of blocks for your quilt size.

UNITS REQUIRED			
	Lap/Twin	Double	Queen/King
Number of pieced square blocks	6	12	21
Number of small hourglass blocks	6	12	21
Number of large hourglass blocks	6	15	30
Number of setting triangle units	14	20	26

1. To make a pieced square block, select 2 matching rectangles A and B and 1 contrasting square C. Sew rectangles A to opposite sides of square C and press.

2. Sew rectangles B to the remaining sides of the center square and press.

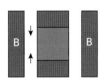

3. Repeat Steps 1 and 2 to make the required number of pieced square blocks.

Pieced square block

4. To make a small hourglass block, select 4 different quarter-square triangles D. Sew the short sides together in pairs. Press. Sew the pairs together and press.

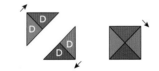

5. Select 2 matching rectangle pairs A and B of a different fabric from the 4 fabrics used in the triangle unit from Step 4. Sew rectangles A to opposite sides of the triangle unit. Press. Sew rectangles B to the remaining sides of the block and press.

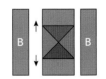

6. Repeat Steps 4 and 5 to make the required number of small hourglass blocks.

Small hourglass block

7. To make a large hourglass block, select 4 different quarter-square triangles E. Sew the short sides together in pairs. Press. Sew the pairs together and press. Repeat to make the required number of large hourglass blocks.

Large hourglass block

8. To make setting triangle units, sew a side setting quarter-square triangle G to 2 sides of a square C. Press. Repeat to make the required number of setting triangle units.

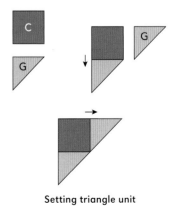

Setting triangle unit

9. Referring to the quilt assembly diagram for your quilt size, arrange large squares F, corner setting triangles H, and all blocks and units on a large design wall. To achieve a well-balanced look, spend time with the arrangement, paying careful attention to the distribution of similar fabrics and light and dark fabrics. Refer to Arranging a Scrappy Quilt, page 14, for additional tips.

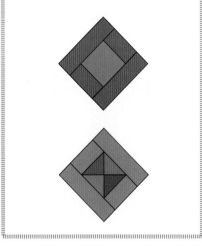

block layout tip

It doesn't matter if you rotate the small hourglass blocks and pieced square blocks. The seams can head in any direction.

10. Referring to the Double quilt assembly diagram, sew the units together into diagonal rows. Press. Sew the rows together to make the center of your quilt. Press the seams in one direction.

border assembly

1. Sew the inner border strips together end-to-end to form 1 long strip. Press the seams open.

2. Refer to Adding Borders, page 18, to measure and trim inner border strips and sew them to the quilt top. Press the seams toward the borders, being careful to get a straight border seam.

3. Repeat Step 2 for the outer borders.

4. Layer, baste, and quilt as desired. Bind and add a label.

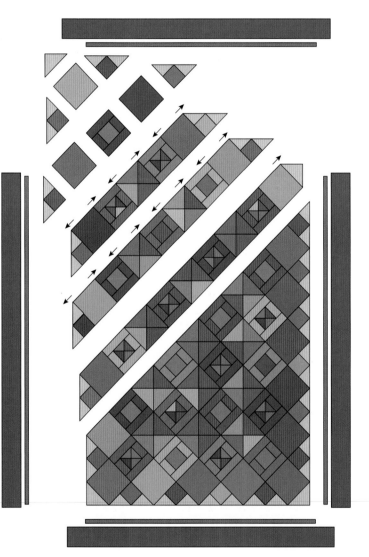

Double quilt assembly diagram

Lap/Twin quilt assembly diagram

Queen/King quilt assembly diagram

Falling Ginkgo Leaves

Wallhanging, 21½" × 37"
Designed, pieced, and quilted by Laurie Shifrin.

Ginkgo leaves intrigue jewelers, visual artists, photographers, and quilters alike. The smooth, fan-shaped leaves resemble butterfly wings, giving them an exotic allure. Ginkgo trees are native to China, where the oldest known living tree is over 3,000 years old. I've seen dozens of them lining the streets of Manhattan—they always give me a warm feeling in that busy place.

Falling Gingko Leaves was inspired by this note card given to me by a friend. I love the composition with its rich colors and unusual background, and nature, as a theme, always appeals to me.

Another source of inspiration was this handwoven wallet I purchased last year for a friend. I loved the unusual color combination so much that I had to buy her another gift so I could keep the wallet as inspiration for a future quilt's color scheme. *Falling Gingko Leaves* was the perfect project for those colors. In this quilt, the rich, moody "bricky" rusts and golds signify the end of the growing season, while in *Early Gingko Leaves*, the second version,

the spring pastels give a feeling of lightness and new growth.

The small size of these quilts was an invitation for me to hand quilt both versions, but I could imagine machine quilting this project using shiny rayon or variegated threads. As for the appliqué, I believe in choosing the technique that best suits each individual project. For this quilt, I show English paper piecing, but because the leaf shapes are simple, you can use any method you prefer.

Note that although both quilts are pictured hanging in one direction, you can rotate them 90°, 180°, or 270° for the look you like best.

Early Ginkgo Leaves
Wallhanging, 21½" × 37"
Designed, pieced,
and quilted by Laurie Shifrin.

fabric tip

For the leaves, I used just one fabric that was pretty consistent throughout, making all the leaves look the same, but it would be fun to use a batik that had more color variation or even to use more than one fabric for the leaves.

fabric placement tip

I intentionally placed the less interesting fabrics, texture-wise, under the leaf appliqués so the leaves would stand out without interference. The fabrics with more pattern or design were used where they could be featured. Notice that I used fabrics of similar weight (value) on the top and bottom.

fabric requirements

Fabric	Wallhanging (21½" × 37")
Background A, B, C, and F	¼ yard each
Background D and E	¼ yard each or 2 fat quarters
Background G	⅓ yard
Leaves	1 fat quarter or regular ¼ yard
Binding	½ yard
Backing	⅞ yard
Batting	28" × 43"

additional requirements

- 2 manila file folders *or* 4 sheets of 8½" × 11" card stock for templates

- Appliqué needles (I recommend Clover Gold Eye appliqué, size 12.)

- Appliqué thread (I recommend YLI silk for invisible stitches.)

- Thimble with indented top (optional but recommended)

- Needle and strong hand-quilting thread for basting

cutting instructions

Refer to the quilt assembly diagram, page 31, for the placement of fabrics.

For	Cut
A	8½" × 25½"
B	7½" × 25½"
C	1" × 25½"
D	6" × 7½"
E	6" × 18½"
F	4" × 21½"
G	8½" × 21½"
Leaves	Will be cut later
Binding	4 strips, 2½" × fabric width

quilt assembly

Use a ¼" seam allowance.

1. Sew rectangles A and B together along the long edges. Press the seam toward the darker fabric.

2. To prepare appliqué templates, trace each of the 4 ginkgo leaves individually, page 36–39, onto separate pieces of white printer paper (or make a photocopy of each template page). Use paper scissors to rough cut each leaf approximately ½" from the traced line. Tape each leaf to a manila folder or card stock and cut out each leaf on the line (do not add a seam allowance). Label the underside of each template with the leaf number and mark it as the wrong side.

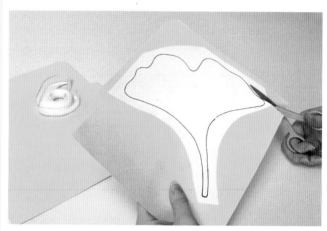

Trace, tape, and cut templates.

3. Pin each leaf template to the wrong side of the leaf fabric with the wrong side of the template up, so you can see the label. Use fabric scissors to rough cut the fabric at least ½" outside the template edge. Leave the fabric pieces pinned to the templates.

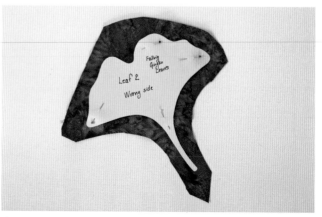

Place template on fabric.

4. Thread a hand sewing needle and knot the thread. Place the knot on the template side of the fabric/template unit and use long stitches (about 1/2" long) to baste each leaf template to the fabric, stitching approximately 1/2" in from the edge. Baste along the length of the stem.

5. Carefully cut the fabric 1/4" from the template edge.

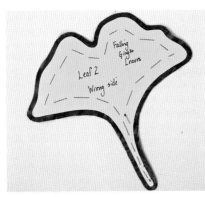

Cut fabric 1/4" from template.

6. Use your fingers to turn under the seam allowance. Baste the raw edges under, placing the knot on the fabric side and sewing through all 3 layers (seam allowance, template, and fabric).

To baste around tight outside curves, such as the points of a leaf, place a small running stitch in the seam allowance and pull the thread to gather the fabric around the curve. You don't need to baste the gathered area to the template, just continue along. Use this same technique to get around the bottom of the stem.

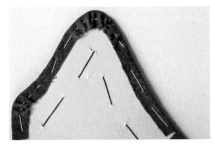

Outside curves

To baste around the inside curves, you may need to clip the seam allowance. Clipping may not be necessary for gentle curves—first try folding them under without clipping. For the deeper curves, use small, sharp scissors to clip a few times along the curve, just shy of the template.

Inside curves

Continue with a running stitch around the entire leaf. To finish basting, knot the thread or tack a backstitch (stitch in place). Placing these basting knots on the right sides of the leaves will make it easier to remove the basting thread later on.

Baste under seam allowance on stem.

7. After all 4 leaves are basted, settle the seam allowances by pressing each leaf on the wrong side with a hot steam iron. As you move the iron, lift instead of sliding, to avoid disturbing the seam allowance. Flip each leaf over and press again.

8. Once the leaves have cooled completely, clip both sets of the basting thread in a few places and remove it (I like to leave the basting

thread in the areas I have gathered). Remove the template—the fabric will hold its shape!

9. Referring to the quilt photo, page 32, place the leaves on the background. You can vary where you put the leaves to suit yourself (I like to try different arrangements). Pin in place.

10. Hand baste along the edge of each leaf, approximately 1/8" from the edge. Basting will ensure that the leaves lie flat and that the seam allowances stay turned under as you appliqué each leaf.

11. Use matching thread to appliqué each leaf to the background with a small (short) blind hemstitch. Starting from the back of the work, come up through the background and the very edge of the leaf. Go back down into the background directly across from where your stitch came up and come up through the background and leaf edge again, about 1/8" away. Continue until you have stitched all the way around the leaf. Knot the thread securely on the wrong side of the background (silk thread tends to slip, so knot a few times).

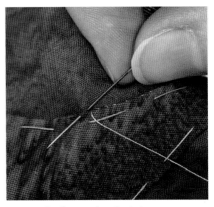

Baste to background and stitch.

12. Once you have appliquéd all 4 leaves, remove the basting stitches and press.

13. Referring to the quilt assembly diagram, finish assembling the quilt top by sewing rectangle C to rectangle B. Press the seam toward C. Sew rectangles D and E together, press the seam in one direction, and then sew the unit to rectangle C. Press the seam toward C. Add top and bottom rectangles F and G. Press the seams toward F and G.

Leaf 1

Ginkgo appliqué template patterns; seam allowances not included.

14. Layer, baste, and quilt as desired.
Bind and add a label.

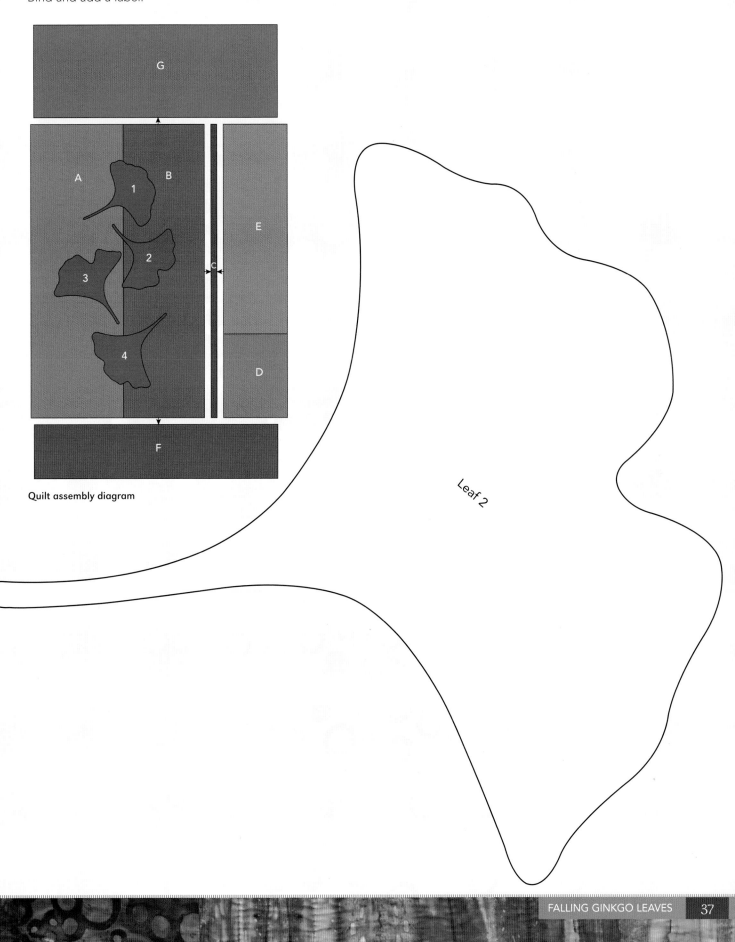

Quilt assembly diagram

Leaf 2

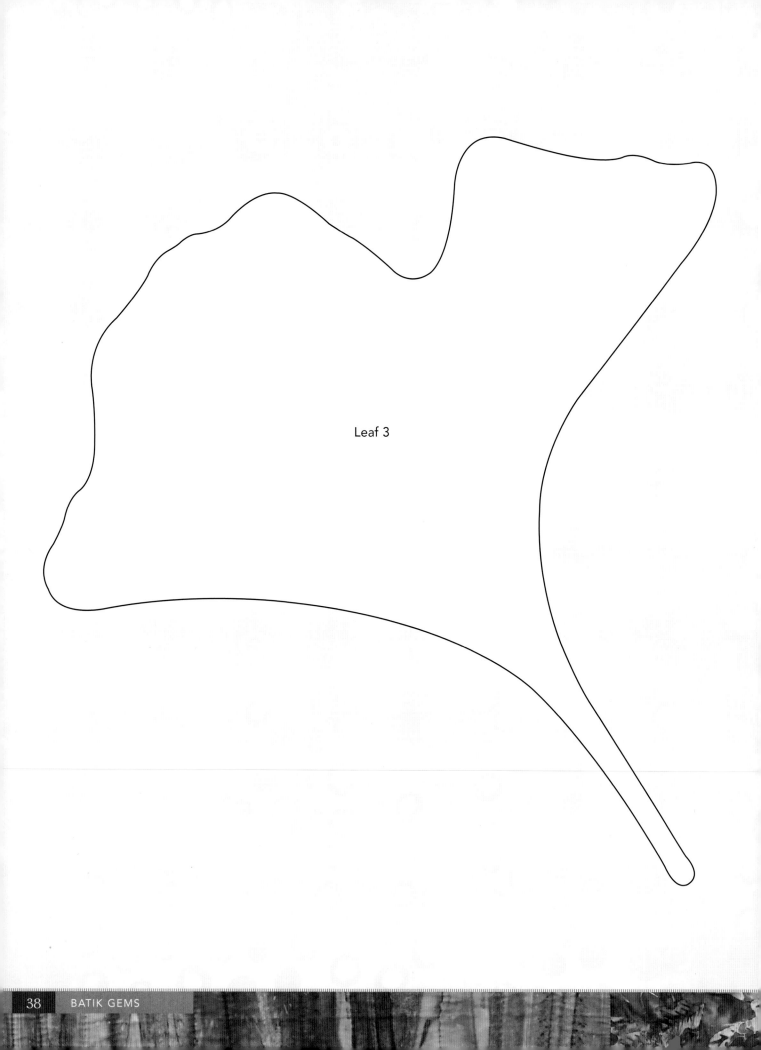

Leaf 3

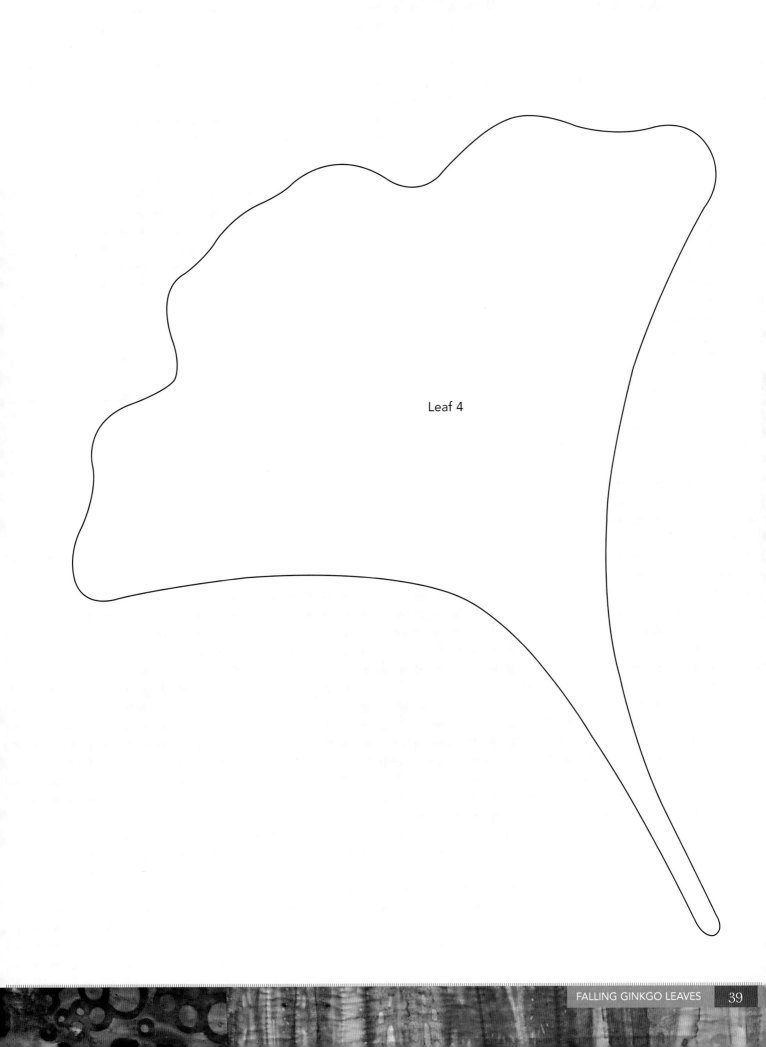

Leaf 4

Phinney Ridge

54½" × 60½". Designed, pieced, and quilted by Laurie Shifrin.

One day while driving down Phinney Avenue, which runs along the top of Phinney Ridge (a Seattle neighborhood near the zoo), I spotted an old graffiti-marked building whose façade had an intriguing brick pattern and a hand-drawn sign on the window.

Photo by Laurie Shifrin

Upon closer inspection, I saw that the sign read "Bricks for sale. Building to be demolished." I took pictures of the brick edifice and went home to design this quilt, incorporating the pattern of the bricks as I created. Within two weeks, the building was gone, making way for yet another group of condos or townhouses, but I had what turned out to be my favorite quilt in this book.

I had been hording this amazing Asian print fabric and, months before, had collected the other fabrics, with no pattern in mind. I used two of my favorite colors, teal and funky green, and I get a warm feeling when I look at this quilt.

More recently, I acquired the two main fabrics in the second quilt, *Living Layers*, the petroglyph print and the pine tree print, both in earth tones, which are my other favorite colors. Now that I've made these two quilts, I can't decide which I like better!

The quilt looks intricate yet is amazingly easy to piece. The fabric selection can be a fun challenge, and I recommend that you have extra fabrics as options. The fabric you choose for the large diamond needs to be an attention-getter. The outer border should feel like a frame, and the rest of the fabrics should complement those two fabrics. I hope you love your quilt as much as I do mine.

Living Layers
54½" × 60½"
Designed, pieced, and quilted by Laurie Shifrin.

fabric requirements

Fabric	Quilt (54½" × 60½")
Multicolored Asian print for large diamonds	1 yard*
Teal/green print for large outer borders	1⅜ yards
Dark teal tonal for large triangles	⅜ yard
Teal tonal for small rectangles surrounding diamonds	½ yard
Light sage tonal for triangles surrounding diamonds	½ yard
Mustard tonal print for thin strips	½ yard
Olive tonal for wide strips	¾ yard
6 or more pale sage/yellow fabrics for bars	¼ yard each
6 or more medium dark fabrics for small squares	⅛ yard each
Binding	⅝ yard
Backing	3¾ yards
Batting	61" × 67"

*Extra fabric allows for selective cutting, but if you use a directional print, you'll need 1¼–1½ yards.

additional requirements

- Acrylic ruler with a 45° line marked on it (Most Omnigrid rulers have this line.)
- 1 sheet template plastic for selective cutting of main Asian print (optional)
- Fine-tipped, black permanent marker (optional)

cutting instructions

For	Cut

NOTE: The number in parentheses is the quantity to cut. Pieces are cut in order of size, largest to smallest.

From multicolored Asian print *

I	(9), 9" × 9"

From teal/green print

S	4 strips, each 9½" × fabric width. Crosscut each strip into (1), 9½" × 21½".

From dark teal tonal

Q	1 strip, 6⅞" × fabric width. Crosscut strip into (2), 6⅞" × 6⅞", then ◻ to make 4 △ plus
N	(2), 3⅞" × 3⅞", then ◻ to make 4 △.

From teal tonal

G	1 strip, 3½" × fabric width. Crosscut strip into (4), 3½" × 6⅞".
M	1 strip, 2" × fabric width. Crosscut strip into (4), 2" × 6⅞".

From light sage tonal

L	1 strip, 5⅜" × fabric width. Crosscut strip into (4), 5⅜" × 5⅜", then ◻ to make 8 △.
H	1 strip, 3⅞" × fabric width. Crosscut strip into (10), 3⅞" × 3⅞", then ◻ to make 20 △.

From mustard tonal print

R	(6), each 2" × fabric width. Crosscut strips into (4), 2" × 21½" plus
E	(4), 2" × 11" plus
F	(2), 2" × 9½", and
K	(8), 2" × 6⅞"

From olive tonal

D	(6), each 3½" × fabric width. Crosscut strips into (4), 3½" × 11" plus
C	(6), 3½" × 9½", and
J	(16), 3½" × 6⅞"

From 6 or more pale sage/yellow fabrics	
B	(40 total), 2" × 8"❋
A	(12 total), 2" × 6½"❋

From 6 or more medium dark fabrics (can use olive and teal leftovers in this mix)	
O	(2 total), 2⅜" × 2⅜", then ◩ to make 4 ◺
P	(64 total), 2" × 2"❋

❋You may wish to cut a few extra to give you choices later on.

From binding fabric	
Binding	(7), 2½" × 40"

◩ = cut square diagonally to make half-square triangles
◺ = half-square triangles

cutting tip for multicolored asian fabric

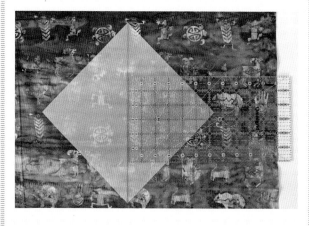

Because the squares in this quilt are on point, if your fabric is directional you may need to cut the squares on the bias so they are facing the right direction in the quilt. The easiest way to do this is to cut a 9" square out of template plastic. On the template, mark one of the diagonals with a dark, fine-tipped permanent marker. When you place the template on the fabric, make sure the drawn line is parallel to the selvage. When you are satisfied with the block, mark around all four sides of the template with a pencil. Cut on the pencil line with scissors or a rotary cutter. **Note: All the edges of your squares are now bias edges. Be careful not to stretch or overhandle them.**

For nondirectional prints, use the above technique for selective cutting on the straight grain but keep one edge of the template parallel to the selvage.

quilt assembly

Use a ¼" seam allowance. Press the seams in the direction of the arrows.

layout tip

Referring to the quilt assembly diagram, page 46, place all your pieces on a design wall before piecing. Using a design wall allows you to become familiar with which fabric belongs where and to audition other fabrics. You can also rearrange large squares I, bars A and B, and small squares P to get a well-balanced, well-distributed placement.

1. Piece together 6 rectangles A. Press the seams in one direction. Repeat to make 2 sets. Sew a rectangle C to the top and bottom of each set. Press. Make 2.

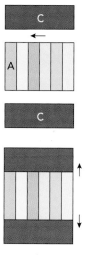

Make 2.

2. Piece together 7 rectangles B. Press the seams in one direction. Repeat to make 4 sets. Sew a rectangle D to one side of each set and a rectangle E to the opposite side. Press. Make 4.

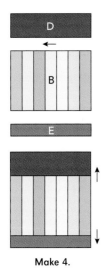

Make 4.

3. Piece together 6 rectangles B. Press the seams in one direction. Repeat to make 2 sets. Sew a rectangle C to one side and a rectangle F to the opposite side of each set. Press. Make 2.

Make 2.

4. Align the 45° line of an acrylic ruler with the top of each rectangle G, J, K, and M and align the edge of the ruler with the point of the rectangle. Trim a triangle off one end of each piece. Trim half the pieces in one direction and half in the other.

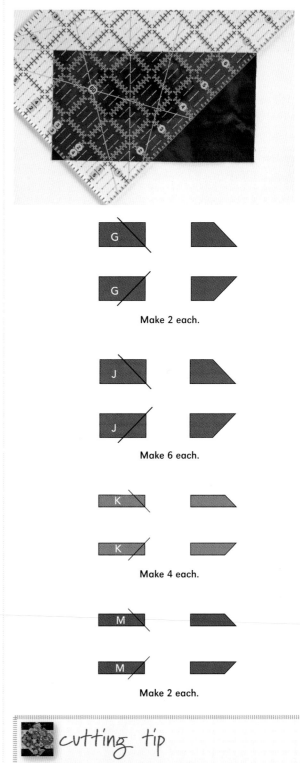

Make 2 each.

Make 6 each.

Make 4 each.

Make 2 each.

cutting tip

If your fabrics don't have right and wrong sides, you can cut all these pieces in one direction.

5. Sew a triangle H to each G piece and press. Sew GH units to opposite sides of a large square I. Press the seams away from the square. Sew GH units to the remaining 2 sides and press.

Make 2 each.

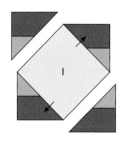

Make 1.

6. Sew a triangle H to each J piece and press. Sew 2 HJ units to opposite sides of large squares I. Press the seams away from the squares. Sew HJ units to the remaining 2 sides and press.

Make 6 each.

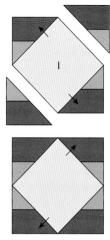

Make 2.

7. Sew a triangle L to each K piece and press. Sew a KL unit and an HJ unit to opposite sides of 4 large squares I. Press the seams away from the squares. Sew a KL unit and an HJ unit to the remaining 2 sides and press.

Make 4 each.

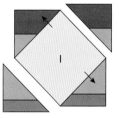
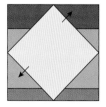

Make 4.

8. Sew together 2 small squares P and a small triangle O. Press the seams toward O. Repeat to make 2 units. Make 2 units with the triangle O facing the other direction. Sew a triangle N and rectangle M to each of the PPO units. Press.

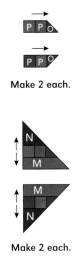

Make 2 each.

Make 2 each.

9. Sew a unit from Step 8 and a triangle Q to opposite sides of 2 large squares I. Press the seams away from the squares. Sew units from Step 8 and a triangle Q to the remaining 2 sides and press.

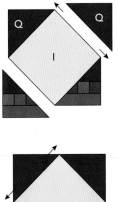

Make 2.

10. Sew 14 small squares P together into 1 long strip. Press the seams in one direction. Repeat to make 4 strips. Sew each of these pieced strips to a long strip R and a large rectangle S. Press. If your S fabric is directional, pay careful attention because 2 of these border units will be turned upside down.

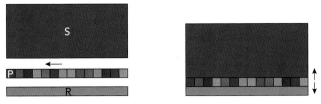

Make 4.

11. Arrange all your assembled parts on your design wall. Once you are sure everything is in the correct place, sew the parts into horizontal rows. Press the seams away from the large I square units. Sew the rows together and press the seams away from the center.

12. Layer, baste, and quilt as desired. Bind and add a label.

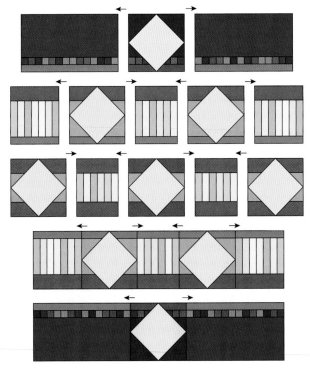

Quilt assembly diagram

The Queen Charlottes

Double, 67¾" × 81"

Designed and pieced by Laurie Shifrin. Quilted by Carrie Peterson.

finished quilt sizes

Crib, 41¼" × 54½"

Lap/Twin, 59¾" × 73" (same as Double but with narrower borders)

Double, 67¾" × 81"

Queen, 88¼" × 101½"

King, 108¾" × 101½"

Finished Block Size: 7¼"

One of the many pleasures of being an author of quilting books has been the opportunity to teach in places I might never have traveled to otherwise. The most spectacular location I've visited is the Queen Charlotte Islands, 80 miles off the coast of British Columbia, Canada, due west of Prince Rupert. The landscape is gorgeous, the views are spectacular, and the women are colorful, to say the least. For six months of the year, the men are off at their jobs in the fishing or lumber industries, giving the women freedom to live as they choose. What has evolved is a kind of raucous camaraderie I've not seen elsewhere.

I was given a full-day tour of the two major islands that make up The Charlottes, as they are called by the locals. In addition to seeing eagles, red-tailed hawks, and fresh bear droppings (thankfully there were no close encounters with any bears), I visited an area known as the mushroom forest, which is pictured here.

What you see are stumps of huge trees, now covered in 4-inch-thick moss, which has smoothed out their surfaces, making them look like huge mushrooms. The color and texture of the moss underfoot inspired this quilt.

The Sprinkler's On!
Crib, 41¼" × 54½"
Designed and pieced by Laurie Shifrin.
Quilted by Carrie Peterson.

fabric requirements

Fabric	Crib (41¼"× 54½")	Lap/Twin (59¾"× 73")	Double (67¾"× 81")	Queen (88¼"× 101½")	King (108¾"× 101½")
Assorted fabrics for Snowball blocks and side and end triangle units	½ yard each of 8 or more fabrics	¾ yard each of 10 or more fabrics	¾ yard each of 10 or more fabrics	1⅛ yard each of 10 or more fabrics	1⅓ yards each of 10 or more fabrics
Multicolored border fabric	1⅝ yards	2⅛ yards	2¾ yards	3½ yards	4⅛ yards
Binding	½ yard	¾ yard	¾ yard	⅞ yard	1 yard
Backing	3 yards	4 yards	5⅛ yards	8½ yards	9½ yards
Batting	48" × 61"	66" × 79"	74" × 87"	95" × 108"	115" × 108"

cutting instructions

Note: Before beginning, read Successful Scrappy Quilts, page 10. I recommend that you cut more of each piece (except from the border fabric) and that you make extra blocks and extra triangle units. You will have leftovers at the end, but the extra pieces will give you the flexibility to eliminate fabrics that don't work as well and to use proportionally more of the ones you really like. Sometimes it's impossible to tell what works until you get the blocks put together.

For	Cut	Crib (41¼" × 54½")	Lap/Twin (59¾" × 73")	Double (67¾" × 81")	Queen (88¼" × 101½")	King (108¾" × 101½")
From assorted fabrics						
E	11½" × 11½", then ⊠	1 total ☐ to make 4 △ (you'll use 2)	2 total ☐ * to make 8 △ (you'll use 2 from each fabric)	2 total ☐ * to make 8 △ (you'll use 2 from each fabric)	2 total ☐ * to make 8 △ (you'll use 3 from each fabric)	3 total ☐ * to make 12 △ (you'll use 8)
A	7¾" × 7¾"	8 total	23 total	23 total	46 total	59 total
D	7⅝" × 7⅝", then ⊠	7 total ☐ to make 28 △	22 total ☐ to make 88 △	22 total ☐ to make 88 △	45 total ☐ to make 180 △	58 total ☐ to make 232 △
F	6" × 6", then ◻	4 total ☐ to make 8 ◺	6 total ☐ to make 12 ◺	6 total ☐ to make 12 ◺	8 total ☐ to make 16 ◺	10 total ☐ to make 20 ◺
G	4⅛" × 4⅛"	12 total	20 total	20 total	28 total	36 total
C	3¼" × 3¼"	14 total	44 total	44 total	90 total	116 total
Sets** of squares B	2½" × 2½"	8 sets total	23 sets total	23 sets total	46 sets total	59 sets total
Individual squares B for end units	2½" × 2½"	2 total	4 total	4 total	6 total	8 total

* Use a different fabric for each square.
** One set is 4 matching squares.

From multicolored border fabric						
Outer borders	4 lengthwise strips	5½" × 50"	4½" × 68"	8½" × 72"	8½" × 90"	8½" × 112"
Top and bottom inner borders	2 lengthwise strips	2" × 31¼"	2" × 51¾"	2" × 51¾"	2" × 72¼"	2" × 92¾"

From remainder of multicolored border fabric					
H	6⅜" × 6⅜", then ⊠	5 □ to make 20 △	9 □ to make 36 △	9 □ to make 36 △	13 □ to make 52 △	17 □ to make 68 △
I	3½" × 3½", then ◺	4 □ to make 8 ◣	4 □ to make 8 ◣	4 □ to make 8 ◣	4 □ to make 8 ◣	4 □ to make 8 ◣
From binding fabric					
Binding	2½" × fabric width	6	8	8	10	12

◹ = cut square diagonally to make half-square triangles
⊠ = cut square twice diagonally to make quarter-square triangles
□ = squares
◺ = half-square triangles
△ = quarter-square triangles

quilt assembly

Use a ¼" seam allowance. Press the seams in the direction of the arrows.

Refer to the block chart below for the required number of blocks for your quilt size.

UNITS REQUIRED					
	Crib	**Lap/Twin**	**Double**	**Queen**	**King**
Number of Snowball blocks	8	23	23	46	59
Number of side triangle units	14	44	44	90	116
Number of end triangle units	2	4	4	6	8
Number of squares G in each pieced border	6	10	10	14	18

BLOCK ASSEMBLY

1. To make Snowball blocks, pair sets of 4 matching small squares B with a large square A of a different fabric. When pairing, consider the following:

❋ Choose pairings that enhance the large squares. You can choose another value of the same color or a different color.

❋ There should be medium contrast between the 2 fabrics, whether in color or value.

❋ If you have a light big square, don't choose equally light corner squares. This will undoubtedly stick out in the final arrangement. Likewise, avoid dark with dark.

❋ If you have many similar fabrics, such as the lavenders in *The Sprinkler's On!*, page 48, spread them out by combining them with the other fabrics instead of with each other.

2. With a sharp number 2 pencil, mark the diagonal on the wrong side of each small square B (see the Technique Tip, page 68).

Mark diagonal on wrong side.

3. Place a square B on a corner of a square A, right sides together. Stitch through both thicknesses along the diagonal marked line (see Accuracy Tip, page 51). Repeat for all 4 corners of square A. Press the square flat.

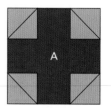

Stitch on marked lines.

accuracy tip

I find that if I stitch just to the right of the marked line, the finished square will be more accurate after pressing.

4. Trim ¼" from the stitched line. Press the triangles open. Referring to the Units Required chart, make the required number of Snowball blocks for your quilt size.

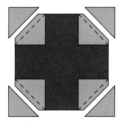

Trim ¼" from stitching line.

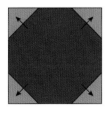

Snowball block

SIDE AND END TRIANGLE UNITS

1. Choose 2 matching triangles D and 1 square C of a different fabric.

color transition tip

When using fabrics with color variations, set the fabrics in their final arrangement before sewing. Look for the best use of the triangles to get the smoothest transition at the seamline.

Bad arrangement

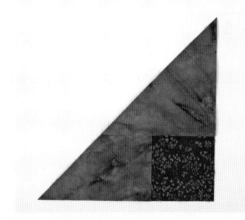

Good arrangement

2. With the square on top, stitch the square to a triangle D as shown. Press the seam toward the square.

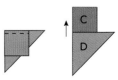

Sew square to triangle.

3. After pressing, align the 3¼" line on your ruler with the left edge of the unit. Trim off the triangle.

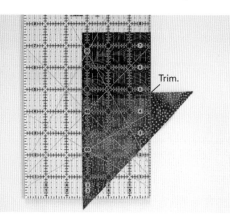

Trim.

---

triangle tip

I know many people save leftover trimmed triangles to turn into quarter-square triangle units for some future miniature project. Feel free to save them in a baggie—if you don't want them, pass them along to a quilting friend. She may consider them a treasure! (I personally throw them away.)

---

4. Pin and sew the trimmed square/triangle unit to the remaining triangle D as shown. Press. Referring to the Units Required chart, page 50, make the required number of side triangle units for your quilt size.

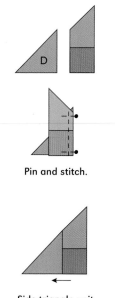

Pin and stitch.

Side triangle unit

---

5. Referring to the quilt assembly diagram for your quilt size, pages 54–55, place all the Snowball blocks and side triangle units on your design wall. Read Successful Scrappy Quilts, page 10, for tips on the best arrangement.

6. Once you are satisfied with the arrangement, choose and place end triangles E on the even columns and corner triangles F on the odd columns. To complete each end triangle unit, remove a triangle E, choose 1 of the remaining squares B, and stitch it to the 90° corner of the triangle, as described in Steps 3–4, pages 50–51. Place the unit back on the wall.

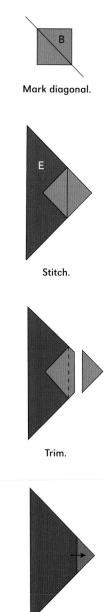

Mark diagonal.

Stitch.

Trim.

End triangle unit

7. Using the diagrams below and the quilt assembly diagram for your quilt size, pages 54–55, as guides, stitch the parts into columns. Press everything in one direction. Sew the columns together to form the center of the quilt top. Press.

 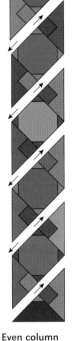

Even column

Odd column

border assembly

1. Referring to the Double and Lap/Twin quilt assembly diagram, page 54, pin a 2" border strip to the top and bottom of the quilt. Stitch with the border strips on top. Press the seams toward the borders.

2. On your design wall, arrange the squares G into 2 strips, aiming for a varied color placement. Refer to the Units Required chart, page 50, for the correct number of squares needed for your quilt size.

 fabric coordination tip

If any of the squares G blend so well with the border fabric that they are barely visible, replace them with different squares G. Any square in which the fabric distracts from the overall effect should also be replaced.

3. Place the border triangles H and I around the squares as shown. Sew the pieces together into HGH units and sew an IGH unit for each end of the border as shown. Press the seams toward the triangles. Sew the units together and add the last 2 triangles I to the ends. Press the seams away from the center.

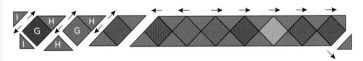

Make 2 pieced border strips (Double and Lap/Twin sizes shown).

4. Sew the pieced borders to the top and bottom of the quilt. Press the seams toward the 2" border strips.

5. Refer to Adding Borders, page 18, to measure and trim the side outer-border strips. Sew the strips to the sides of the quilt. Press the seams toward the borders. Repeat for the top and bottom outer borders.

6. Layer, baste, and quilt as desired. Bind and add a label.

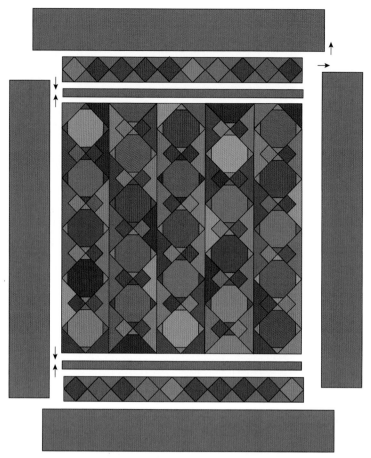

Double and Lap/Twin quilt assembly diagram (Lap/Twin has narrower borders than shown.)

Crib quilt assembly diagram

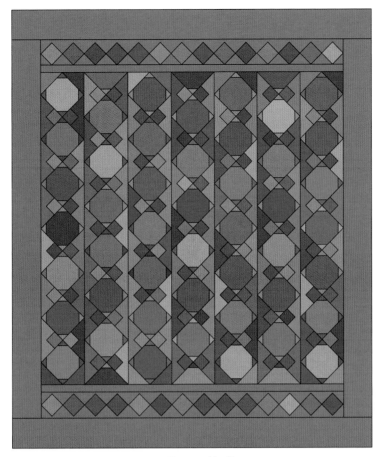

Queen quilt assembly diagram

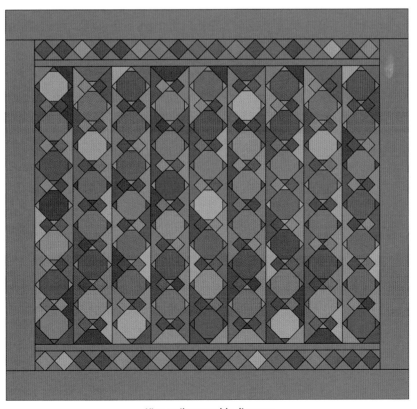

King quilt assembly diagram

Broken Garden Path

Crib/Wallhanging, $39\frac{1}{2}" \times 36\frac{1}{2}"$
Designed, pieced, and quilted by Laurie Shifrin.

After taking a class with Reynola Pakusich, author of *Circle Play*, I fell in love with circles—I can't get enough of them. I travel a lot, and my favorite projects to bring on airplanes are circles waiting to be appliquéd. They are easy and transportable, and they get done fast. Recently, I saw a gorgeous quilt my friend Diane Roubal had made—full of circles. I had quilt envy! The result—*Broken Garden Path*.

This wallhanging introduces you to my favorite easy technique for appliquéing circles, and it gives *you* the chance to be a designer. Use the exact same layout I did or rearrange the pieces to make your own creation. Directions are for the quilt as you see it, but, really, go for it and create your own original wallhanging.

I've provided directions for one size (Crib/Wallhanging), but you can make a larger quilt by adding borders, or you can double the size of each piece (finished size × 2 plus ½" seam allowance) to get a quilt that is 78½" × 72½" (Twin/Double).

For your feature print, choose a medium- to large-scale multicolored print. The quilt will be more interesting if there is variation across the fabric, rather than a repeated pattern. Florals and Asian prints work great, as do large-scale batiks; and if there's a fabric with a highlight color or value contrast (like the white in my Asian fabric), that fabric will surely pop compared to the others.

fabric selection tip

Not all your coordinating fabrics should be eye-catchers. This would overwhelm the main fabric, and the quilt would get too busy. Choose some tonals or one-color batiks that feel like background fabrics or blenders. Choose some small-scale prints or batiks. The fabrics should mesh to form a collage, and the main print should be the attention-getter. Notice that I used three fabrics that are almost the same chartreuse/olive green and four fabrics that are dark teal/blue. This helps to give continuity throughout the quilt.

Color Blast
Crib/Wallhanging, 39½" × 36½"
Designed, pieced, and quilted by Laurie Shifrin.

fabric requirements

Fabric	Wallhanging (39½" × 36½")
Feature print	1 yard *
12 or more coordinating fabrics	⅜ yard each
Binding	½ yard
Backing	1⅜ yards
Batting	43" × 46"

* *Extra fabric allows for selective cutting, but if you use a directional print, you'll need $1\frac{1}{4}$ yards.*

additional requirements

- 1 sheet of template plastic for circle templates
- Graphite or white marking pencil
- Fine-tipped, black permanent marker (optional)
- Awl or similar pointed object
- Freezer paper (found next to the aluminum foil in most grocery stores)
- Sharp needles or appliqué needles (I recommend Clover Gold Eye appliqué, size 12.)
- Appliqué thread (I like YLI silk.)
- Thimble with indented top (optional but recommended)
- Needle and strong hand-quilting thread for basting

cutting instructions

For	Cut
NOTE: The number in parentheses is the quantity to cut. Pieces are cut in order of size, largest to smallest.	
Feature print *	
Featured rectangle	(1), 9½" × 12½"
Featured square	(1), 9½" × 9½"
Featured rectangle	(1), 6½" × 12½"
Featured square	(1), 6½" × 6½"
Small squares	(7), 3½" × 3½"

* *Aim for a variety of looks from each of the 4 larger pieces. Be sure to include some of the highlight colors, that is, the ones that catch the eye.*

For	Cut
5 coordinating fabrics	
Large circle background squares	(1 each), 6½" × 6½"
8 coordinating fabrics	
Small squares **	(1 each), 3½" × fabric width. Crosscut each strip into (11), 3½" × 3½".

** *You will cut extra small squares so you have choices for placement.*

For	Cut
2 different coordinating fabrics	
Four-patches	(2 each), 2" × fabric width
2 more coordinating fabrics	
Four-patches	(1 each), 2" × fabric width
Binding fabric	
Binding	(5), 2½" × fabric width

NOTE: Large and small circles will be cut later.

quilt assembly

Use a ¼" seam allowance. Press the seams in the direction of the arrows.

1. To make four-patch units, stitch together the pairs of 2" strips. You'll make 2 strip sets from 2 of the fabrics, and 1 strip set from the remaining 2 fabrics. Press the seams toward the darker fabrics.

2. Crosscut each strip set into 2" segments, 24 of one combination and 18 of the other. Stitch the segments together in pairs to produce four-patches. Press the seams in one direction. You'll need 12 four-patches from the first pair of fabrics and 9 from the other pair. Save any extras for possible alterations you may choose to make to the design.

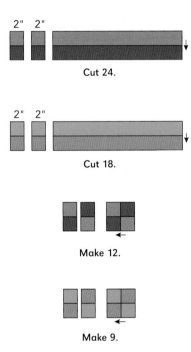

2" 2"

Cut 24.

2" 2"

Cut 18.

Make 12.

Make 9.

3. Referring to the quilt assembly diagram, page 63, arrange all squares, four-patches, and pieces of the feature print on the design wall. You will have extra 3½" squares, which you can use if you want to change the arrangement.

Spend a little time moving the like-size pieces around to get the best color and value balance. Refer to Successful Scrappy Quilts, page 10, for tips. You can, of course, vary from my layout. The easiest way is to swap 3" finished squares for other 3" finished squares or swap 6" finished squares for 4 of the 3" finished squares. Beyond that, the math gets tricky.

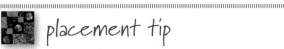

placement tip

Once you are pleased with the arrangement, take a digital photo. As you remove pieces from the design wall, you can refer to the photo to return them to the same place.

MAKING THE CIRCLE UNITS

1. On the right side of each square that will have a circle appliqué, mark the center with a graphite or white marking pencil. Find the center by measuring 3¼" *in* and 3¼" *down* on the large squares and 1¾" *in* and 1¾" *down* on the small squares.

2. Select fabrics for the circles. You'll need 5 different large circles A, and you'll need 22 small circles B in matching groups of 7, 5, 5, 3, and 2. You can include the feature print in your fabric selections for the circles.

3. To make the circle appliqués, you can use your preferred appliqué method or follow these directions for my favorite technique for easy circles. **Note:** I've described English paper piecing appliqué in the directions for *Falling Ginkgo Leaves*, pages 34–35, if you'd like to try a different technique.

4. Place template plastic over the printed circle template patterns, page 63, and trace with a fine-tipped permanent marker. Mark the center point. Use paper scissors to cut out the template plastic on the traced line. Use an awl to make a hole large enough for a pencil tip at the center mark of each template. Label each piece. **Note:** The template patterns do not include seam allowances.

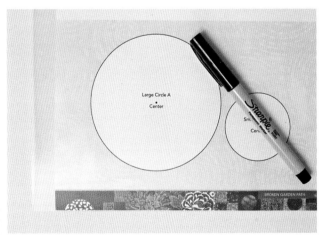

5. Cut 5 squares 5" × 5" and 22 squares 3" × 3" from freezer paper.

6. To cut circles, you can cut up to 4 layers of freezer paper at a time. Stack the layers dull side up, shiny side down. On the top layer trace the large circle A on the 5" squares and the small circle B on the 3" squares. Staple the layers together just inside the traced lines to prevent the paper from shifting while you cut.

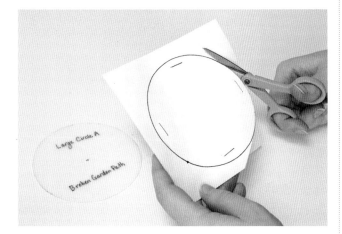

7. Cut out the circles on the traced lines and remove the staples. Mark the center on the dull side of each circle.

8. Place the shiny side of a freezer paper circle face down on the wrong side of a circle fabric. With a hot, dry iron (no steam), press the paper circle onto the fabric. The freezer paper will take about 2 seconds to stick. Leave at least 1" between circles on the same fabric. Keep the freezer paper attached to the fabric until you are finished with the appliqué.

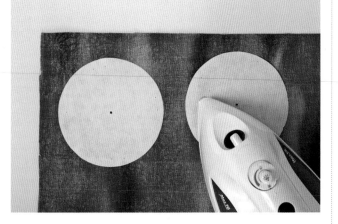

9. Use fabric scissors to cut out the fabric circles. Cut ¼" outside the paper edge for the seam allowance.

10. Stick a straight pin through the center mark of a fabric circle and align it with the center mark on the corresponding background square. This process will center the circle on the background square.

11. Pin the circle in place. Baste the circle in place, approximately ⅝" in from the edge. Remove the pins.

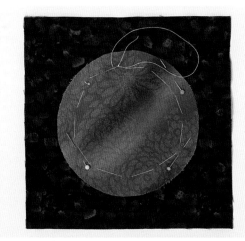

12. To appliqué, use a sharp or an appliqué needle and fine (silk) thread. (Refer to the Thread Tip, page 36, for a knotting trick.) Use your needle to turn under the raw edge of the fabric, just to the edge of the freezer paper. Take a few stitches using a small (short) blind hemstitch; starting from the back, come up through the background and the folded edge of the circle. Go back down into the background directly across from where your stitch came up and then come up again ⅛" away, again through the background and the edge of the circle. After every stitch or 2, use the needle to turn under more seam allowance. Continue until you have gone all the way around the circle.

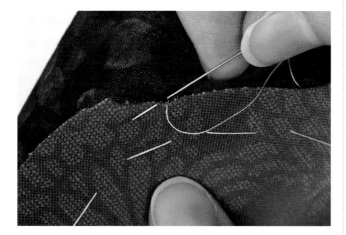

13. After you've sewn around the entire edge, knot the thread securely on the back (silk tends to slip, so knot a few times). Remove the basting stitches. Use small, sharp scissors, on the wrong side of the fabric, to carefully make a slit through the background fabric only (1½" on large circles and 1" on small circles). Remove the freezer paper, using tweezers if necessary. You may have to give it a gentle tug if you've stitched through the paper.

14. Repeat Steps 10–13 to appliqué all of the circles that were cut.

ASSEMBLING THE GROUPS

1. Refer to the quilt assembly diagram, page 63. Note how the quilt can be divided into groups of pieces. Assemble each of the groups, following the diagrams below. Press the seams in the direction of the arrows.

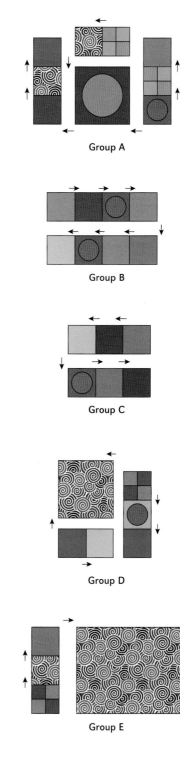

Group A

Group B

Group C

Group D

Group E

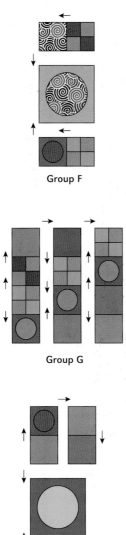

Group F

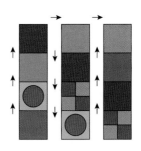

Group J

Group G

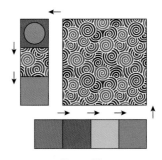

Group K

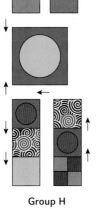

Group H

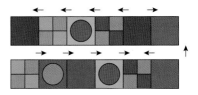

Group L

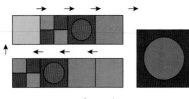

Group I

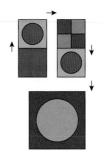

Group M

Group N

2. Sew the groups together in the following sequence and press the seams in the direction of the arrows.

Group A to Group B

Group C to Group D

Group F to Group G

Group J to Group K

Group M to Group N

Group AB to Group CD

Group E to Group FG

Group H to Group EFG

Group I to Group JK

Group L to Group MN

Group ABCD to Group EFGH

Group IJK to Group LMN

3. Sew the 2 halves together. Press.

4. Layer, baste, and quilt as desired. Bind and add a label.

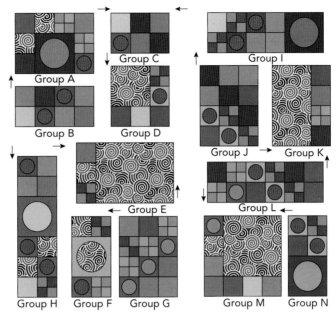

Quilt assembly diagram

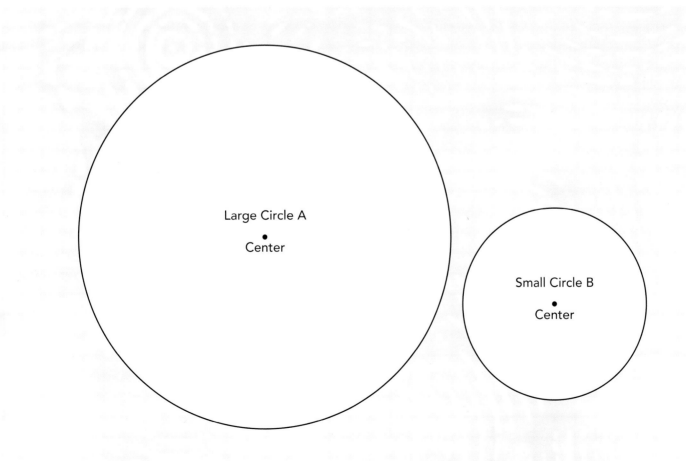

Large Circle A
● Center

Small Circle B
● Center

Coral Fantasy

Double/Queen, 81⅛" × 101"
Designed and pieced by Laurie Shifrin. Quilted by Carrie Peterson.

finished quilt sizes

Crib, 53¼" × 53¼"
(narrower 5" border)
Lap, 61¼" × 61¼"
Twin, 61¼" × 81⅛"

Double/Queen, 81⅛" × 101"
King, 101" × 120⅞"
Finished Star Block: 12"

When I first began quilting, I loved creating my own blocks and making them in earthy colors and a scrappy style with a repeated block setting. After 28 years, nothing has changed! The inspiration for this quilt comes from one of my earliest quilts—it's actually the only quilt I have hanging in my home. This particular star block has a great deal of complexity to it. The potential for variation is huge, and that's why I like it! You'll notice that my early quilt hangs unevenly along the bottom. For some reason, I added an extra triangle unit on the bottom border. Somehow I made it fit, but it'll never hang straight!

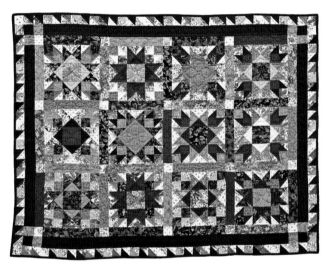

Walking around my neighborhood in the spring as each flower and tree comes into bloom provided the inspiration for the colors for this quilt. Two of my favorites are the delicate pink poppy and the salmon-colored dogwood. When I went to my fabric stash, I was surprised to find I had a nice range of these colors. For the border, a multicolored batik would have worked, but I chose this rich cranberry hand-dyed fabric, which showcases each of the star blocks.

Although I used just one color group—pinky coral—this quilt would be stunning in a wide variety of colors and values as in the smaller quilt, *Summer Celebration*. The stars are still scrappy, but you'll notice the sashing and border accents are all one fabric, as are the setting triangles.

Here are some tips for making your fabric selection easier and for using your fabrics to maximum effect:

✿ Don't be afraid to use prints in this quilt. The prints in *Coral Fantasy* are subtle enough not to distract from the overall effect, but in *Summer Celebration*, I have lots of fun, busy prints.

✿ You'll notice that none of the darker-value fabrics are in the sashing and setting triangles or in the small squares of the border. At first, I tried using the full range of fabric values, but I found the darks to be distracting. An alternate choice would have been to use the mediums and darks for the sashing and the lights for the setting triangles.

✿ First, make one complete star block to get a full understanding of the steps. The block should measure 12½" from edge to edge. If it is too large or too small, you'll need to adjust your seam allowance. See my tip on page 16 regarding scant ¼" seam allowances. Next, make all your star point units; then make the corner units. On a design wall, match the star centers and the centers of the units to get the most variety.

✿ *Coral Fantasy* has only six dark fabrics. When it came time to place the units, I tried to include at least one of these fabrics in each block so that none of the blocks appeared too light or washed out.

Summer Celebration, Crib, 53¼" × 53¼"
Designed, pieced, and quilted by Laurie Shifrin.

fabric requirements

Fabric	Crib (53¼" × 53¼")	Lap (61¼" × 61¼")	Twin (61¼" × 81⅛")	Double/Queen (81⅛" × 101")	King (101" × 120⅞")
Medium/light fabrics for star blocks, sashing, border accents, and setting triangles	⅞ yard each of 4 or more	⅞ yard each of 4 or more	1 yard each of 4 or more	1 yard each of 8 or more	1⅜ yards each of 8 or more
Medium and medium/dark fabrics for star blocks	⅜ yard each of 4 or more	⅜ yard each of 4 or more	½ yard each of 4 or more	⅝ yard each of 6 or more	¾ yard each of 8 or more
Medium/dark fabric for cornerstones (can use border fabric if it's not too busy)	⅛ yard	⅛ yard	¼ yard	¼ yard	½ yard
Border	1¼ yards	2 yards	2⅜ yards	3⅛ yards	3¾ yards
Binding	⅝ yard	⅝ yard	¾ yard	⅞ yard	1 yard
Backing	3⅝ yards	4⅛ yards	5⅛ yards	7⅝ yards	11 yards
Batting	60" × 60"	68" × 68"	68" × 87"	87" × 107"	107" × 127"

cutting instructions

For	Cut	Crib (53¼" × 53¼")	Lap (61¼" × 61¼")	Twin (61¼" × 81⅛")	Double/Queen (81⅛" × 101")	King (101" × 120⅞")

NOTE: The number in parentheses is the quantity to cut. Pieces are cut in order of size, largest to smallest.

From medium/light fabrics

For	Cut	Crib	Lap	Twin	Double/Queen	King
Side setting triangles F	21⅛" × 21⅛", then ⊠	2 □* to make 8 △ (you will use 4)	2 □* to make 8 △ (you will use 4)	2 □* to make 8 △ (you will use 6)	4 □* to make 16 △ (you will use 10)	4 □* to make 16 △ (you will use 14)
Corner setting triangles G	12¼" × 12¼", then ◺	2 □** to make 4 ◿	2 □** to make 4 ◿	2 □** to make 4 ◿	2 □** to make 4 ◿	2 □** to make 4 ◿
Sashing E	2½" × 12½"	16	16	24	48	80
Border accent I	2½" × 2½"	8	8	10	14	18

* Cut each from a different fabric.
** Cut each from a different fabric and do not use the same fabrics as in side setting triangles.

From remainder of medium/light, medium, and medium-dark fabrics

	Cut	Crib	Lap	Twin	Double/Queen	King
A	5¼" × 5¼"	5 sets of 2***	5 sets of 2***	8 sets of 2***	18 sets of 2***	32 sets of 2***
A	5¼" × 5¼"	10	10	16	36	64
D	4½" × 4½"	5	5	8	18	32
B	2⅞" × 2⅞"	10 sets of 4***	10 sets of 4***	16 sets of 4***	36 sets of 4***	64 sets of 4***
C	2½" × 2½"	10 sets of 4***	10 sets of 4***	16 sets of 4***	36 sets of 4***	64 sets of 4***

*** One set is made from pieces of the same fabric.

From cornerstone fabric						
C		(1), 2½" × fabric width. Crosscut strip into (12), 2½" × 2½".	(1), 2½" × fabric width. Crosscut strip into (12), 2½" × 2½".	(2), 2½" × fabric width. Crosscut strips into (17), 2½" × 2½".	(2), 2½" × fabric width. Crosscut strips into (31), 2½" × 2½".	(4), 2½" × fabric width. Crosscut strips into (49), 2½" × 2½".
From border fabric						
M		(4), 5½" × 15½"	(4), 9½" × 19½"	(4), 9½" × 19½"	(4), 9½" × 19½"	(4), 9½" × 19½"
K		(4), 5½" × 17½"	(4), 9½" × 17½"	(6), 9½" × 17½"	(10), 9½" × 17½"	(14), 9½" × 17½"
L		(4), 5½" × 10½"	(4), 9½" × 10½"	(4), 9½" × 10½"	(4), 9½" × 10½"	(4), 9½" × 10½"
J		(8), 2⅝" × 3⅜"	(8), 3⅜" × 6⅝"	(10), 3⅜" × 6⅝"	(14), 3⅜" × 6⅝"	(18), 3⅜" × 6⅝"
H	2⅜" × 2⅜", then ◰	16 □ to make 32 ◺	16 □ to make 32 ◺	20 □ to make 40 ◺	28 □ to make 56 ◺	36 □ to make 72 ◺
From binding fabric						
Binding	2½" × fabric width	6	7	8	10	12

◩ = cut square diagonally to make half-square triangles
⊠ = cut square twice diagonally to make quarter-square triangles
□ = squares
◺ = half-square triangles
△ = quarter-square triangles

block assembly

Use a ¼" seam allowance. Press the seams in the direction of the arrows.

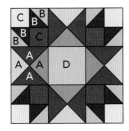

1. To make one complete star block, make star points, choose 4 squares A: 2 identical and 1 each of 2 different fabrics. Arrange the squares in pairs, right sides together, so that you have 1 of the identical squares in each pair. With a sharp number 2 pencil and a ruler, mark the diagonal on the wrong side of the lighter fabric in each pair. Stitch ¼" from each side of the marked line. Press flat.

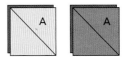

Place right sides together and mark diagonal.

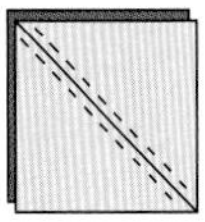

Stitch ¼" from each side of marked line.

technique tip

Hold the pencil at an angle of about 40° to the table. This angle not only will prevent you from snagging or stretching the fabrics but will also sharpen the pencil as you go.

2. Cut on the *unmarked* diagonal; then cut on the marked diagonal. Press the seams of all units toward the identical fabric.

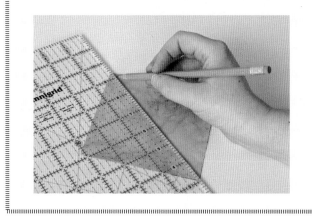

Cut first on unmarked diagonal.

Then cut on marked diagonal line.

3. Arrange the triangle units as shown and sew 4 star point units. Press the seams in one direction.

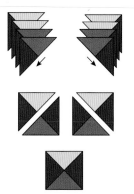

Make 4 star point units.

4. To make corner units, choose 2 sets of 4 identical squares B. Arrange them in pairs, right sides together. Mark the diagonal, stitch, and press as you did in Step 1.

5. Cut only on the *marked* diagonal. Press the seams toward the darker fabric. Make 8.

Stitch 4.

Cut on diagonal.

Make 8.

6. Choose 2 different sets of 4 identical squares C. The squares should be of different fabrics from those you have already used. Sew the squares to the triangle units from Step 5 in pairs together using 1 square from each set. Make 4 corner units. Press.

Make 4 each.

Make 4 corner units.

7. Choose a star center D and arrange the star point units, the corner units, and the center square. Remember that you can rotate the star point units and the corner units 180° for a different effect. Once you are pleased with the arrangement, stitch the units together to make 1 complete star block. Refer to the tips on page 65 to check the measurement of the block.

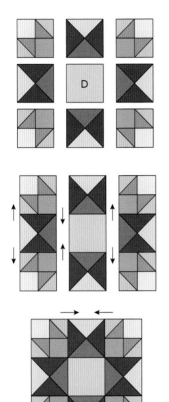

Star block

STAR BLOCKS AND BORDER UNITS REQUIRED					
	Crib	Lap	Twin	Double/Queen	King
Star blocks	5	5	8	18	32
Border accent units	8	8	10	14	18

8. Referring to the Star Blocks and Border Units Required chart, repeat Steps 1–7 to make the required number of star blocks for your quilt size. To help with fabric placement, read the tips on page 65. Aim for a variety of looks in your blocks, referring to the quilt photos on pages 64 and 65 and the diagrams below for ideas.

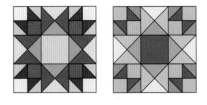

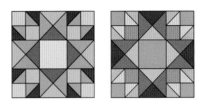

quilt assembly

1. Referring to the quilt assembly diagram for your quilt size, pages 70–72, arrange the star blocks, sashing rectangles E, cornerstones C, side setting triangles F, and corner setting triangles G on the design wall.

Adjust the various parts to get a pleasing arrangement. Refer to Arranging a Scrappy Quilt, page 14, and the tips below.

✿ Similar stars should be distributed evenly around the quilt. These may be stars in which the center square or the star points are the most noticeable.

✿ Distribute the darkest fabrics evenly.

✿ Make sure the sashing rectangles E aren't directly adjacent to the same fabric in the star blocks or the setting triangles.

2. Stitch the sashing/cornerstone rows together. Press the seams toward the sashing rectangles. Stitch the sashing/star block rows together. Press the seams toward the sashing rectangles.

3. Sew the sashing strips to star strips in the order shown. Sew the side setting triangles to the rows. Press the seams away from the triangles. Sew the rows together. Sew the corner setting triangles to the quilt. Press the seams toward the triangles.

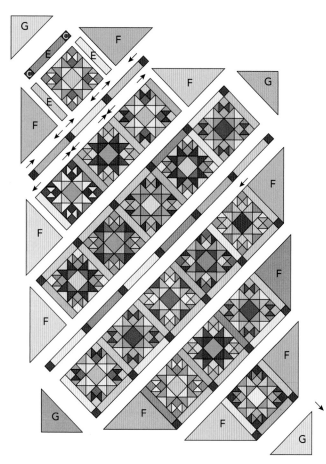

Double/Queen quilt assembly diagram

border assembly

1. To make an accent unit, choose 1 border accent square I and 4 triangles H. Sew triangles to opposite sides of the square. After pressing, sew the other 2 triangles to the remaining sides of the square. Sew a rectangle J to one side of the new square.

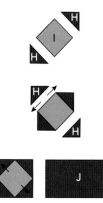

2. Make the required number of accent units for your quilt size (refer to the chart on page 69).

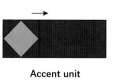

Accent unit

3. Referring to the quilt assembly diagram for your quilt size, pages 70–72, place rectangles K, L, and M and the accent units on the design wall, around the center of the quilt top. Once you are pleased with the placement of the accent units, sew 2 side borders and borders for the top and bottom of the quilt. Shown at right are the borders for the Double/Queen size. Press the seams toward the large rectangles.

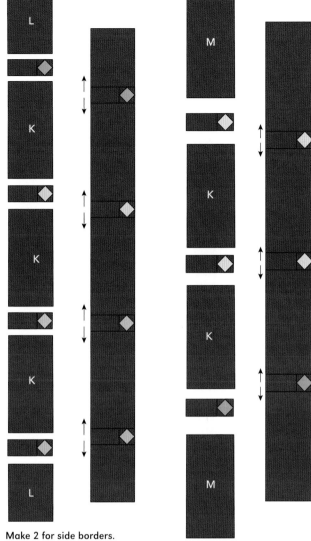

Make 2 for side borders.

Make 2 for top and bottom borders.

4. Referring to Adding Borders, page 18, pin and sew the side borders to the quilt. Press the seams toward the borders. Sew the top and bottom borders to the quilt. Press the seams toward the borders.

5. Layer, baste, and quilt as desired. Bind and add a label.

Crib and Lap quilt assembly diagram

Note: *The only difference between the Crib and Lap sizes is the width of the borders.*

Twin quilt assembly diagram

Double/Queen quilt assembly diagram

King quilt assembly diagram

Crossroads

Lap/Twin, 63" × 73"

Designed and pieced by Laurie Shifrin. Quilted by Carrie Peterson.

finished quilt sizes

Crib, 44¼" × 51¼"

Lap/Twin, 63" × 73"

Double, 75½" × 87½"

Queen, 88" × 102"

King, 100½" × 116½"

Quilt designs that radiate from the center have always intrigued me. They have symmetry and a center focal point like flowers such as dahlias and daisies. These quilts can be as simple as a Trip Around the World quilt or as complex in design as this one. The bonus with *Crossroads* is that the piecing is as easy as it gets—squares and rectangles.

Fabric selection plays an important role in the overall outcome. This design uses nine fabrics for the chains, six more for the background, and one for the outer border and binding. In *Crossroads*, the background is made up of three different prints for each of the large blue and green background areas.

To make a version with fewer fabrics, you have a few options. *Rainy Days Don't Get Me Down*, shows how you can use one fabric for Fabrics 10, 11, and 12 and another for Fabrics 13, 14, and 15. Just pick fabrics that are pretty enough or interesting enough to use in large quantities. If you aren't using batiks, novelty prints or Asian prints will work well.

For the small chain squares, a variety of colors is necessary, but you can repeat some of the fabrics. Just buy

enough to experiment at home. (See the Fabric Buying Tip, page 75.) Choose fabrics that are one-color textures or tonals and that stand out against Fabrics 10–15. If they are too busy (prints) or too "blendy," the dimensional effect of the design will not show.

Rainy Days Don't Get Me Down
Crib, 44¼" × 51¼"
Designed, pieced, and quilted by Laurie Shifrin.

fabric requirements

Fabric	Crib (44¼" × 51¼")	Lap/Twin (63" × 73")	Double (75½" × 87½")	Queen (88" × 102")	King (100½" × 116½")
Fabric 1 for center square	2¼" × 2¼"	3" × 3"	3½" × 3½"	4" × 4"	4½" × 4½"
Fabric 2 for chain squares	¼ yard	½ yard	½ yard	½ yard	¾ yard
Fabric 3 for chain squares	¼ yard	¼ yard	¼ yard	⅓ yard	⅓ yard
Fabric 4 for chain squares	¼ yard	¼ yard	¼ yard	⅓ yard	½ yard
Fabric 5 for chain squares	¼ yard	¼ yard	⅜ yard	½ yard	⅝ yard
Fabric 6 for chain squares	¼ yard	¼ yard	⅜ yard	½ yard	⅝ yard
Fabric 7 for chain squares	¼ yard	⅓ yard	½ yard	½ yard	¾ yard
Fabric 8 for chain squares	¼ yard	⅓ yard	½ yard	½ yard	¾ yard
Fabric 9 for chain squares	¼ yard	½ yard	⅝ yard	⅝ yard	⅞ yard
Fabric 10 for background	⅓ yard	½ yard	⅝ yard	¾ yard	¾ yard
Fabric 11 for background	½ yard	⅝ yard	¾ yard	⅞ yard	1⅛ yards
Fabric 12 for background	⅞ yard	1¼ yards	1¾ yards	2¼ yards	3¼ yards
Fabric 13 for background	⅓ yard	½ yard	½ yard	⅝ yard	¾ yard
Fabric 14 for background	⅓ yard	½ yard	¾ yard	⅞ yard	1⅛ yards
Fabric 15 for background	½ yard	⅞ yard	1⅛ yards	1⅛ yards	1⅜ yards
Fabric 16 for border	⅔ yard	1½ yards	1¾ yards	2⅛ yards	2⅝ yards
Binding	½ yard	¾ yard	⅞ yard	1 yard	1 yard
Backing	3⅛ yards	4¾ yards	7¼ yards	8¼ yards	10¾ yards
Batting	51" × 58"	69" × 79"	82" × 94"	94" × 108"	107" × 123"

fabric buying tip

You may choose to rearrange the order of the small square chain fabrics, so I recommend buying the largest amount required for each of these fabrics. The extra yardage will give you the option of making adjustments. For Fabrics 3–9, consider buying ½ yard each for the Lap/Twin size, ⅝ yard each for the Double size, ⅝ yard each for the Queen size, and ⅞ yard each for the King size.

HOW TO USE THE CUTTING CHARTS

Use the Number of Pieces to Cut chart to determine how many of which pieces of fabric you'll need. Refer to the Measurements of Pieces chart, page 76, to get the size for each piece in your quilt size. Fabric 1 is easy—you need only 1 square for the center of the quilt. For Fabric 2, you need 28 small squares A. To get this number of squares, you'll have to cut strips the width of the square (according to the chart). For the Crib size, that would be 2¼"-wide strips.

To cut fabrics that are used for more than one size of piece and to cut all rectangles, start by cutting the largest piece needed for that fabric (working back from E to A). The most efficient way to do this is to cut a strip as wide as the *first* measurement of the largest piece. For example, for Fabric 11 of the Double size, you need 2 rectangles C, which measure 6½" × 9½", so cut a 6½"-wide strip (not a 9½"-wide strip). Crosscut the strip into rectangles 9½" in length. Continue by cutting the next largest pieces from the remainder of the strip.

organization tip

Use a highlighter to mark the column that has the piece for your quilt sizes. Notice that A is the smallest piece and E is the largest.

cutting instructions

MEASUREMENTS OF PIECES

NOTE: The number in parentheses is the quantity to cut. Pieces are cut in order of size, largest to smallest.

Piece	Crib (44¼" × 51¼")	Lap/Twin (63" × 73")	Double (75½" × 87½")	Queen (88" × 102")	King (100½" × 116½")
Small square A	2¼" × 2¼"	3" × 3"	3½" × 3½"	4" × 4"	4½" × 4½"
Large square B	4" × 4"	5½" × 5½"	6½" × 6½"	7½" × 7½"	8½" × 8½"
Small rectangle C	4" × 5¾"	5½" × 8"	6½" × 9½"	7½" × 11"	8½" × 12½"
Large rectangle D	7½" × 9¼"	10½" × 13"	12½" × 15½"	14½" × 18"	16½" × 20½"
Border rectangle E	4" × 19¾"	5½" × 28"	6½" × 33½"	7½" × 39"	8½" × 44½" (cut lengthwise)
Binding	(5), 2½" × fabric width	(8), 2½" × fabric width	(9), 2½" × fabric width	(11), 2½" × fabric width	(12), 2½" × fabric width

NUMBER OF PIECES TO CUT

NOTE: The number of pieces is the same for all quilt sizes.

Fabric	Small square A	Large square B	Small rectangle C	Large rectangle D	Border rectangle E
Fabric 1	1	—	—	—	—
Fabric 2	28	—	—	—	—
Fabric 3	8	—	—	—	—
Fabric 4	10	—	—	—	—
Fabric 5	18	—	—	—	—
Fabric 6	18	—	—	—	—
Fabric 7	26	—	—	—	—
Fabric 8	26	—	—	—	—
Fabric 9	34	—	—	—	—
Fabric 10	12	—	2	—	—
Fabric 11	18	4	2	—	—
Fabric 12	20	4	8	4	—
Fabric 13	10	—	2	—	—
Fabric 14	18	4	2	—	—
Fabric 15	26	8	2	—	—
Border 16	8	—	—	—	8

quilt assembly

Use a ¼" seam allowance. Press the seams in the direction of the arrows.

1. Referring to the quilt assembly diagram, page 79, place all the cut pieces on a design wall. If you're making a large size and don't have room for the whole quilt on the wall, do a quarter of the quilt at a time. Once the pieces are up, step back to make sure you like the arrangement. Look specifically at the small chain squares (Fabrics 3–9). You can swap the small chain square fabrics, aiming for a good balance between the squares heading left and right and the squares heading up and down. Once you are happy with the arrangement, make a fabric key using the model below.

Crossroads Fabric Key

Fabric 1   Fabric 10
Fabric 2   Fabric 11
Fabric 3   Fabric 12
Fabric 4   Fabric 13
Fabric 5   Fabric 14
Fabric 6   Fabric 15
Fabric 7   Border 16
Fabric 8   Binding
Fabric 9

Fabric key

3. The remaining sections will each be made twice: once for the top half of the quilt and again for the bottom half. Use the method described in Step 2 to assemble 2 vertical center rows.

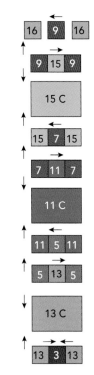

Vertical center row; make 2.

fabric tip

If your Fabrics 10–15 vary noticeably across the fabric, like those in Rainy Days Don't Get Me Down, *try to place similarly colored pieces adjacent to each other.*

Bad placement

Good placement

2. Referring to your fabric key and the diagram below, assemble the horizontal center row. Sew the small squares A together into units of 3. Press. Sew the AAA units to the rectangles C. Press.

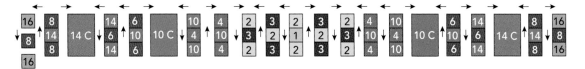

Horizontal center row; make 1.

4. Referring to the diagrams below, assemble 2 each of Section A and Section A reversed, Section B and Section B reversed, Section C and Section C reversed, and Section D and Section D reversed. Press as you go, following the pressing arrows on the diagrams.

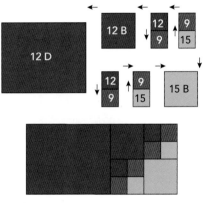

Make 2 Section A.

Make 2 Section A reversed.

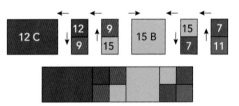

Make 2 Section B.

Make 2 Section B reversed.

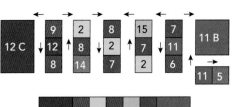

Make 2 Section C.

Make 2 Section C reversed.

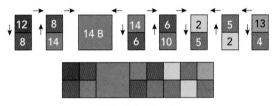

Make 2 Section D.

Make 2 Section D reversed.

5. Referring to the quilt assembly diagram, sew Sections A–D and Sections A–D reversed together. Add border rectangles E to the side of each unit, then to the top of each unit. You will now have 2 quadrants and 2 reversed quadrants.

6. Sew a vertical center row between a quadrant and a reversed quadrant. Repeat with the remaining quadrants. Sew the top half of the quilt to the horizontal center row. Then sew the bottom half to the other side of the horizontal center row.

7. Layer, baste, and quilt as desired. Bind and add a label.

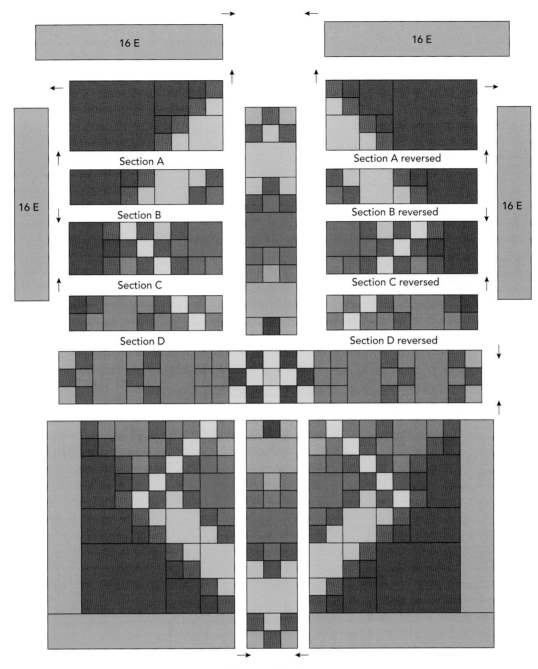

16 E

16 E

16 E

16 E

Section A

Section A reversed

Section B

Section B reversed

Section C

Section C reversed

Section D

Section D reversed

Quilt assembly diagram

Bits & Bars

Double, 70" × 86"
Designed and pieced by Laurie Shifrin. Quilted by Carrie Peterson.

finished quilt sizes

Crib, 46" × 46"
Lap/Twin, 62" × 78"
(same number of blocks
as Double with a
narrower border)

Double, 70" × 86"
Queen, 86" × 86"
King, 102" × 102"
Finished Bar Block Size: 16"

This is the second quilt to be inspired by the scouring rush, pictured on page 21, as well as this ceramic tile created by a wonderful artist in Dublin, Ireland. The tile, like the plant, has vertical lines interrupted by randomly placed black spots.

Tile made by artist Orla Kaminska.

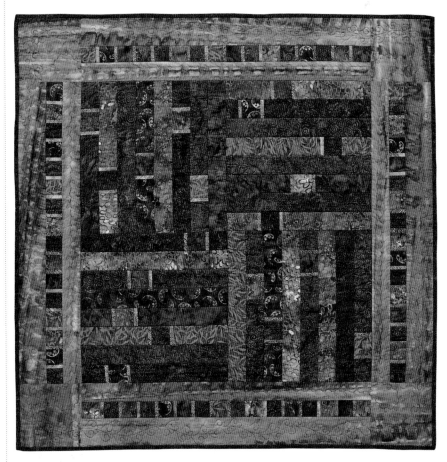

Good Vibrations
Crib, 46" × 46"
Designed, pieced, and quilted by Laurie Shifrin.

fabric note

I used 3 fabrics for the flanges in Bits & Bars *and only 1 fabric in* Good Vibrations. *If you like an even less scrappy look, try using only 1 fabric for all the small squares in the blocks and pieced border sections. I recommend using at least 10 fabrics for the long bars mainly because there are 8 bars per block and it would be much less interesting to have only 8 fabrics, each appearing in every block. Having 10 fabrics allows you to mix it up.*

In *Bits & Bars*, the interruptions are achieved with thin strips made by using flanges, also called faux piping. This technique allows you to make very thin strips without the hassle of sewing very narrow strips. As an added bonus, the flaps add a tactile aspect to the quilt.

When I completed this quilt top, it seemed a little too linear for my taste. Most of my designs have a diagonal aspect or some other quality that draws the eye around the quilt, and this one seemed very "blocky." I worked with my quilter, Carrie, and we decided she would stitch an allover curvy, floral pattern reflecting the shape of the flowers in the border fabric. The quilting really softened the 90° angles and sharp edges. Now when I look at this quilt, it feels much more comfortable.

I took the exact opposite approach with *Good Vibrations*. There was already a lot going on with the bright colors, so I stitched in-the-ditch on the blocks. It just goes to show that there isn't one right way to quilt a quilt, and you should consider your individual tastes when deciding on the quilting designs.

fabric requirements

Fabric	Crib (46" × 46")	Lap/Twin (62" × 78")	Double (70" × 86")	Queen (86" × 86")	King (102" × 102")
10 fabrics for bar blocks and border squares	¼ yard each	⅝ yard each	⅝ yard each	⅔ yard each	1 yard each
3 fabrics for flanges	¼ yard each	⅜ yard each	⅜ yard each	⅜ yard each	½ yard each
Border	1⅛ yards	2 yards	2¾ yards	2⅞ yards	3⅜ yards
Binding	½ yard	¾ yard	⅞ yard	⅞ yard	1 yard
Backing	3⅛ yards	5 yards	5½ yards	8⅛ yards	9⅝ yards
Batting	52" × 52"	68" × 84"	76" × 92"	92" × 92"	108" × 108"

cutting instructions

BAR BLOCKS						
For	Cut	Crib (46" × 46")	Lap/Twin (62" × 78")	Double (70" × 86")	Queen (86" × 86")	King (102" × 102")
From 10 fabrics for bar blocks and border squares						
	2½" × fabric width	2 each	6 each	6 each	7 each	11 each
From above strips (cut in order listed)						
D	2½" × 16½"	12 total	36 total	36 total	48 total	75 total
A	2½" × 15"	20 total	60 total	60 total	80 total	125 total
E	2½" × 2¼"	64 total	112 total	112 total	128 total	160 total
B	2½" × 2½"	20 total	60 total	60 total	80 total	125 total
From 3 fabrics for flanges						
Flanges	1¼" × fabric width	7 total	15 total	15 total	18 total	26 total

BORDERS AND BINDING					
For	Crib (46" × 46")	Lap/Twin✳ (62" × 78")	Double✳ (70" × 86")	Queen✳ (86" × 86")	King✳✳ (102" × 102")
From border fabric					
NOTE: The number in parentheses is the quantity to cut.					
H	(4), 3½" × 32½"	(2), 3½" × 64½" plus (2), 3½" × 48½"	(2), 6¾" × 64½" plus (2), 6¾" × 48½"	(4), 6¾" × 64½"	(4), 6¾" × 80½"
G	(4), 2½" × 32½"	(2), 2½" × 64½" plus (2), 2½" × 48½"	See below.	See below.	See below.
I	(4), 7¼" × 7¼"	(4), 7¼" × 7¼"	(4), 11¼" × 11¼"	(4), 11¼" × 11¼"	(4), 11¼" × 11¼"

✳ From the large piece of border fabric, cut a piece 66" × fabric width. Cut the above pieces lengthwise from that piece.
✳✳ From the large piece of border fabric, cut a piece 82" × fabric width. Cut the above pieces lengthwise from that piece.

From remaining border fabric					
			(6), 3¼" × fabric width	(7), 3¼" × fabric width	(9), 3¼" × fabric width
Piece above strips together end-to-end. From that long strip, cut:					
G			(2), 3¼" × 64½" plus (2), 3¼" × 48½"	(4), 3¼" × 64½"	(4), 3¼" × 80½"
From binding fabric					
Binding	(5), 2½" × fabric width	(8), 2½" × fabric width	(9), 2½" × fabric width	(10) 2½" × fabric width	(11), 2½" × fabric width

quilt assembly

Use a ¼" seam allowance. Press the seams in the direction of the arrows.

1. Fold each of the 1¼"-wide flange strips in half lengthwise, *wrong* sides together. Press well.

Press, wrong sides together.

2. Cut the strips into the required number of 2½" segments C and 2¼" segments F for your quilt size referring to the chart below.

3. Randomly sort the 2½" × 15" rectangles A into 5 stacks, making sure there is a variety of fabrics in each stack. Cut all the rectangles in the stack into 2 pieces at each of the following measurements, keeping the 2 pieces from each rectangle paired together:

7½" from one edge (Stack 1)

6½" from one edge (Stack 2)

5½" from one edge (Stack 3)

4½" from one edge (Stack 4)

3½" from one edge (Stack 5)

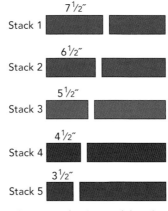

Stack 1 — 7½"
Stack 2 — 6½"
Stack 3 — 5½"
Stack 4 — 4½"
Stack 5 — 3½"

Cut rectangles A at each length, keeping the 2 pieces from each rectangle paired together.

4. Take 2 matching pieces of the 2½" flange segments C, both parts of 1 of the rectangles A, and 1 contrasting square B. Align the raw edges of a flange segment C to a short edge of each of the 2 parts of the rectangle A, right sides together. Baste using a very scant seam allowance (³⁄₁₆" or less).

Baste flange segments to both rectangle A parts.

5. Stitch the square B to both of the flange strips, right sides together. Sew through all 4 layers, using a regular seam allowance and regular stitch length. Carefully press the seams toward the square B so that the flanges are lying on the rectangle A parts. Check that the measurement of the new rectangle is 16½". If not, check your seam allowance and pressing and adjust both before continuing.

Sew to square B.

6. Repeat Steps 4 and 5 for all the rectangles A, mixing and matching the flange and square B fabrics.

---

basting tip

I use a long basting stitch to attach the flange segment to the rectangle A part, and I use a ³⁄₁₆" seam allowance. The sewing, which is only meant to baste the two parts together, goes faster that way. The stitching will be covered by the regular seam used to attach the square B. Don't forget to return to a small stitch length after basting the flanges.

SUBCUTTING FLANGES						
For	**Cut**	**Crib**	**Lap/Twin**	**Double**	**Queen**	**King**
Crosscut the folded flange strips into:						
Segments C for bar blocks *(must be in matching pairs)*	1¼" × 2½" segments	20 pairs (40 total)	60 pairs (120 total)	60 pairs (120 total)	80 pairs (160 total)	125 pairs (250 total)
Segments F for pieced border strips	1¼" × 2¼" segments	60	108	108	124	156

7. To make 1 complete bar block, choose 5 of the pieced rectangles A, cut at different lengths and using different fabrics, and 3 different rectangles D. Arrange the strips to get a pleasing random grouping and sew them together. Make sure the flange/square/flange segments in adjacent strips are spaced so they do not overlap. Press the seams toward the rectangles D when possible; otherwise, press to one side. Use steam if the seam allowances won't lie flat.

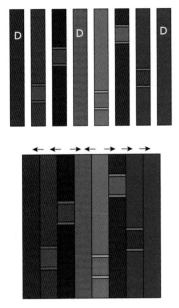

Bar block

placement tip

It's easier if the first and last pieces are rectangles D as in Bits & Bars. *It is also important that the flange/square/flange portions do not overlap.*

8. Repeat Step 7 to make the required number of bar blocks for your quilt size.

BAR BLOCKS REQUIRED					
	Crib	Lap/Twin	Double	Queen	King
Number of bar blocks	4	12	12	16	25

9. Referring to the quilt assembly diagram for your quilt size, pages 85–86, sew the blocks together into rows. Press. Sew the rows together to form the center of your quilt. Press all the seams in one direction.

border assembly

1. To make the pieced portion of the border, sew a flange segment F to a short side of a rectangle E. Repeat to make the number of required EF units for your quilt size.

BORDER UNITS REQUIRED					
	Crib	Lap/Twin	Double	Queen	King
Number of EF units	60	108	108	124	156
Number of EF units in each side border	15	31	31	31	39
Number of EF units in top and bottom borders	15	23	23	31	39

2. Sew the required number of EF units together to make 2 side pieced-border strips and top and bottom pieced-border strips. Distribute the fabrics to get a random look. Sew a rectangle E to the end of each strip so the strips start and end with a rectangle E. Press the seams so the flanges lie the way they were originally sewn (all in one direction).

Make 2 side pieced-border strips and 2 top and bottom pieced-border strips.

3. For the Lap/Twin and Double sizes, pin and sew the longer border strip G to one long side of each side pieced-border strip and sew the longer border strip H to the other long side. Sew the shorter G and H strips to the top and bottom pieced-border strips. Press the seams toward G and H.

For the Crib, Queen, and King sizes, pin and sew a border strip G to one long side of each of the 4 pieced strips and sew an H to the other side. Press the seams toward G and H.

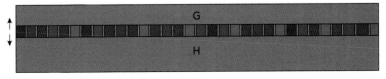

Add longer border strips G and H to side pieced-border strips.

4. For all quilt sizes, sew squares I to either end of the top and bottom pieced-border strips. Press the seams toward the pieced portion.

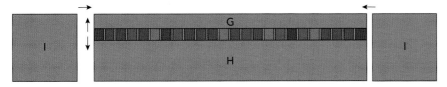

Sew square I to each end of top and bottom pieced-border strips.

5. Pin and sew the side borders to the quilt. Press. Pin and sew the top and bottom borders to the quilt.

6. Layer, baste, and quilt as desired. Bind and add a label.

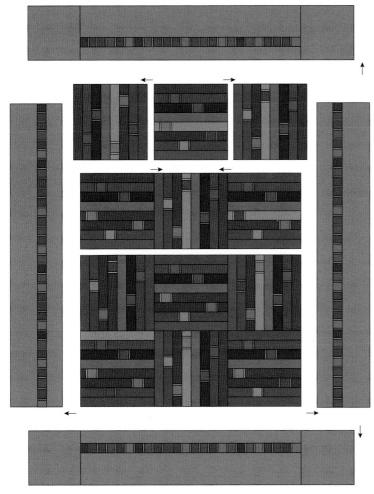

Double and Lap/Twin quilt assembly diagram
(Lap/Twin has narrower borders than shown.)

Crib quilt assembly diagram

Queen quilt assembly diagram

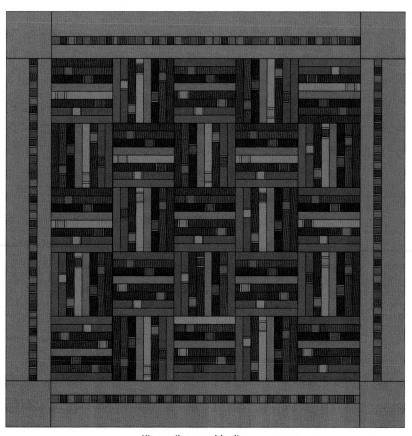

King quilt assembly diagram

Coming Full Circle

Twin/Double, 67½" × 67½"

Designed and pieced by Laurie Shifrin. Quilted by Carrie Peterson.

finished quilt sizes

Crib/Lap, 49½" × 49½"
Twin/Double, 67½" × 67½"
Queen/King, 101" × 101"

Finished Log Cabin Block Size:
Crib/Lap and Twin/Double, 8"
Queen/King, 12"

While shopping for holiday gifts last year, I found this mass-produced small ceramic bowl in a number of kitchen stores. I'd been thinking about making a quilt using the wonderful hydrangea batik seen in the border of *Coming Full Circle* in a Log Cabin pattern. I decided to adapt my original pattern to reflect the circular swirls of the paint pattern on the bowl, incorporating the color combination of chartreuse and periwinkle.

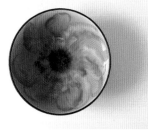

You can emphasize different features of the quilt pattern by varying the values of the fabrics. In *Coming Full Circle*, the circles are clearly formed, and the three chains create a woven texture through the circles. In *Chain Reaction*, the circles are almost indistinguishable and become the background for the two-toned chains. The optical illusions formed by the difference in values make it hard to believe that these quilts are from the same pattern.

The size of most quilts can be changed by adding or subtracting blocks and by increasing or decreasing the size of each piece. In the case of *Coming Full Circle*, both methods were used to create the multiple size options. For the Crib/Lap size, the center portion of the Twin/Double quilt is all that is needed for the complete quilt. For the Queen/King size, the pieces were all enlarged.

A few aspects of this quilt can be changed for a less scrappy look. I used four different dark blues and four different greens for the circles, but you may choose to use just one blue and one green—yardages for both options are provided.

My samples are made entirely out of batiks, but I can envision an elegant and sophisticated version of this quilt in gorgeous Asian fabrics with rich, gold-highlighted prints as the circle fabrics and Asian tonal fabrics for the chains.

Chain Reaction
Crib/Lap, 49½" × 49½"
Designed, pieced, and quilted by Laurie Shifrin.

fabric requirements

Fabric	Crib/Lap (49½" × 49½")	Twin/Double (67½" × 67½")	Queen/King (101" × 101")
Dark blue circles (DB)			
if using 4 fabrics	⅜ yard each	⅜ yard each	⅝ yard each
if using 1 fabric	1⅛ yards	1⅛ yards	1⅞ yards
Green circles (GR)			
if using 4 fabrics	—	⅓ yard each	½ yard each
if using 1 fabric	—	⅞ yard	1⅜ yards
Light blue print circles (except Crib/Lap), outer border, and binding (LB)	1⅝ yards	2⅛ yards	5½ yards
Light periwinkle center background (PW)	—	¼ yard	⅜ yard
Light lavender background on green circles (LV)	—	⅓ yard	½ yard
Purple outer background (PU)	⅜ yard	⅝ yard	1 yard
Light purple big X chain (LP)	⅓ yard	⅜ yard	⅝ yard
Chartreuse diamond chain (CH)	⅓ yard	⅓ yard	½ yard
Medium blue outer chain (MB)	—	½ yard	¾ yard
Teal inner border (TE)	⅓ yard	½ yard	⅝ yard
Backing	3⅜ yards	4½ yards	9⅜ yards
Batting	56" × 56"	74" × 74"	107" × 107"

Fabric key

■	DB	Dark blue circles (4 fabrics for scrappy version)
■	GR	Green circles (4 fabrics for scrappy version)
■	LB	Light blue print circles (same as outer border)
■	PW	Light periwinkle center background
■	LV	Light lavender background
■	PU	Purple outer background
■	LP	Light purple big X chain
■	CH	Chartreuse diamond chain
■	MB	Medium blue outer chain
■	TE	Teal inner border

organization tip

To avoid confusion about which fabric is for what part, make an enlarged photocopy of the fabric key. Cut a small swatch of each of your fabrics and affix the swatches next to their appropriate places on the key.

cutting instructions

Fabric	Crib/Lap (49½" × 49½")	Twin/Double (67½" × 67½")	Queen/King (101" × 101")
Dark blue circles (DB1–4)	3[10], 2½" × fabric width* Crosscut strips into: 8[32], 2½" × 6½" (F) 8[32], 2½" × 3½" (C) 8[32], 1½" × 1½" (A)	3[10], 2½" × fabric width* Crosscut strips into: 8[32], 2½" × 6½" (F) 8[32], 2½" × 3½" (C) 8[32], 1½" × 1½" (A)	3[12], 3½" × fabric width* Crosscut strips into: 8[32], 3½" × 9½" (F) 8[32], 3½" × 5" (C)
	1[4], 1½" × fabric width* Crosscut strips into: 2[8], 1½" × 9½" (H) 2[8], 1½" × 9" (G)	1[4], 1½" × fabric width* Crosscut strips into: 2[8], 1½" × 9½" (H) 2[8], 1½" × 9" (G)	2[8], 2" × fabric width* Crosscut strips into: 2[8], 2" × 14" (H) 2[8], 2" × 13¼" (G) 8[32], 2" × 2" (A)
Green circles (GR1–4)	—	2[7], 2½" × fabric width* Crosscut strips into: 6[24], 2½" × 6½" (F) 6[24], 2½" × 3½" (C)	3[9], 3½" × fabric width* Crosscut strips into: 6[24], 3½" × 9½" (F) 6[24], 3½" × 5" (C)
	—	1[3], 1½" × fabric width* Crosscut strips into: 2[8], 1½" × 9½" (H) 6[24], 1½" × 1½" (A)	1[4], 2" × fabric width* Crosscut strips into: 2[8], 2" × 14" (H) 6[24], 2" × 2" (A)
Light blue print circles, outer border, and binding (LB) (cut in the order given)	4 lengthwise strips, 6½" × 54" for outer border	4 lengthwise strips, 6½" × 72" for outer border	4 lengthwise strips, 9½" × 106" for outer border
	4 lengthwise strips, 2½" × 54" for binding	4 lengthwise strips, 2½" × 72" for binding	(6), 3½" × fabric width Crosscut strips into: (16), 3½" × 9½" (F) (16), 3½" × 5" (C)
	—	(4), 2½" × fabric width Crosscut strips into: (16), 2½" × 6½" (F) (16), 2½" × 3½" (C)	(11), 2½" × fabric width for binding
	—	(8), 1½" × fabric width Crosscut strips into: (4), 1½" × 9½" (H) (12), 1½" × 8½" (I) (16), 1½" × 5½" (E) (16), 1½" × 2½" (B) (16), 1½" × 1½" (A)	(12), 2" × fabric width Crosscut strips into: (4), 2" × 14" (H) (12), 2" × 12½" (I) (16), 2" × 8" (E) (16), 2" × 3½" (B) (16), 2" × 2" (A)
Light periwinkle center background (PW)	(3), 1½" × fabric width Crosscut strips into: (4), 1½" × 8½" (I) (8), 1½" × 5½" (E) (8), 1½" × 2½" (B)	(3), 1½" × fabric width Crosscut strips into: (4), 1½" × 8½" (I) (8), 1½" × 5½" (E) (8), 1½" × 2½" (B)	(4), 2" × fabric width Crosscut strips into: (4), 2" × 12½" (I) (8), 2" × 8" (E) (8), 2" × 3½" (B)
Light lavender background (LV)	—	(4), 1½" × fabric width Crosscut strips into: (8), 1½" × 8½" (I) (8), 1½" × 5½" (E) (8), 1½" × 2½" (B)	(6), 2" × fabric width Crosscut strips into: (8), 2" × 12½" (I) (8), 2" × 8" (E) (8), 2" × 2½" (B)
Purple outer background (PU)	(6), 1½" × fabric width Crosscut strips into: (4), 1½" × 8½" (I) (24), 1½" × 5½" (E) (24), 1½" × 2½" (B)	(11), 1½" × fabric width Crosscut strips into: (8), 1½" × 8½" (I) (40), 1½" × 5½" (E) (40), 1½" × 2½" (B)	(15), 2" × fabric width Crosscut strips into: (8), 2" × 12½" (I) (40), 2" × 8" (E) (40), 2" × 2½" (B)

Fabric			
Light purple big X chain (LP)	(1), 2½" × fabric width Crosscut strip into: (16), 2½" × 2½" (D)	(2), 2½" × fabric width Crosscut strips into: (24), 2½" × 2½" (D) (1), 1½" × 1½" (A)	(3), 3½" × fabric width Crosscut strips into: (24), 3½" × 3½" (D) (16), 2" × 2" (A)
	(2), 1½" × fabric width Crosscut strips into: (33), 1½" × 1½" (A)	(2), 1½" × fabric width Crosscut strips into: (52), 1½" × 1½" (A)	(2), 2" × fabric width Crosscut strips into: (37), 2" × 2" (A)
Chartreuse diamond chain (CH)	(1), 2½" × fabric width Crosscut strip into: (16), 2½" × 2½" (D)	(1), 2½" × fabric width Crosscut strip into: (16), 2½" × 2½" (D)	(2), 3½" × fabric width Crosscut strips into: (16), 3½" × 3½" (D)
	(2), 1½" × fabric width Crosscut strips into: (36), 1½" × 1½" (A)	(2), 1½" × fabric width Crosscut strips into: (36), 1½" × 1½" (A)	(2), 2" × fabric width Crosscut strips into: (36), 2" × 2" (A)
Medium blue outer chain (MB)	—	(2), 2½" × fabric width Crosscut strips into: (32), 2½" × 2½" (D)	(3), 3½" × fabric width Crosscut strips into: (32), 3½" × 3½" (D)
	—	(3), 1½" × fabric width Crosscut strips into: (64), 1½" × 1½" (A)	(4), 2" × fabric width Crosscut strips into: (64), 2" × 2" (A)
Teal inner border (TE)	(4), 1½" × fabric width Crosscut strips into: (4), 1½" × 9½" (H) (12), 1½" × 8½" (I)	(6), 1½" × fabric width Crosscut strips into: (8), 1½" × 17½" (J) (4), 1½" × 9½" (H) (4), 1½" × 8½" (I)	(8), 2" × fabric width Crosscut strips into: (8), 2" × 26" (J) (4), 2" × 14" (H) (4), 2" × 12½" (I)

✳ The number before the bracket is the quantity to cut for each of the fabrics. The number in brackets is the total quantity to cut if you're using only 1 fabric.

cutting tip

Label each group of cut pieces with the respective letter name to avoid confusion when piecing.

log cabin block assembly

For all sizes:

Use a ¼" seam allowance. Press the seams in the direction of the arrows.

Each Log Cabin block is constructed the same way, using different combinations of fabrics. Each piece has a fabric color that can be identified in the fabric key and a letter for the piece size. For instance, to assemble one of the center Log Cabin blocks, you will use light periwinkle center-background pieces B and E; pieces A, C, and F from the dark blue circle fabric (or one of the 4 if you are making the scrappy version); and light purple big-X-chain pieces A and D.

Using the illustrations below as a guide, assemble one center Log Cabin block, pressing in the direction of the arrows after each step.

1. Sew a dark blue square A to a light purple square A. Repeat to get 2 pairs.

2. Sew the pairs together to form a four-patch.

3. Sew a light periwinkle rectangle B to the top of the four-patch, paying attention to the orientation.

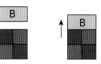

4. Sew a light purple square A to a light periwinkle rectangle B and sew the unit to the block.

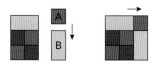

5. Sew a dark blue rectangle C to the other side of the block.

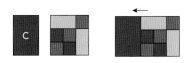

6. Sew a light purple square D to a dark blue rectangle C and add the unit to the bottom of the block.

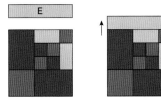

7. Sew a light periwinkle rectangle E to the top of the block.

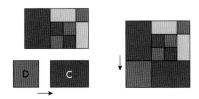

8. Sew a light purple square A to a light periwinkle rectangle E and sew the unit to the right side of the block.

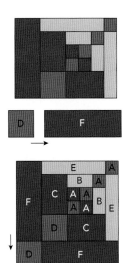

9. Sew a dark blue rectangle F to the left side of the block.

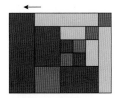

10. Sew a light purple square D to a dark blue rectangle F and sew the unit to the bottom of the block.

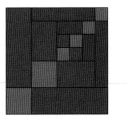

Log Cabin block

You have one completed center Log Cabin block.

FOR CRIB/LAP SIZE

1. Following the Log Cabin block assembly instructions (Steps 1–10), pages 91–92, assemble 3 more center Log Cabin blocks identical to the one just made.

2. Repeat these steps to make 4 Log Cabin blocks using fabrics as shown in the diagram below.

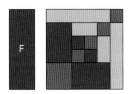

Make 4 using dark blue circle fabrics, light purple chain fabric, and purple outer background fabric (1 with each dark blue fabric for scrappy version).

3. Repeat to make 8 Log Cabin blocks using fabrics as shown in the diagram below.

Make 8 using dark blue circle fabrics, chartreuse chain fabric, and purple outer background fabric (2 with each dark blue fabric for scrappy version).

FOR TWIN/DOUBLE AND QUEEN/KING SIZES

1. Following the Log Cabin block assembly instructions (Steps 1–10), pages 91–92, make 3 more center Log Cabin blocks identical to the one completed in Step 10.

2. Repeat these steps to make 4 Log Cabin blocks using fabrics as shown in the diagram below.

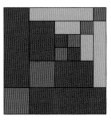

Make 4 using dark blue circle fabrics, light purple chain fabric, and light lavender background fabric (1 with each dark blue fabric for scrappy version).

3. Repeat to make 8 Log Cabin blocks using fabrics as shown in the diagram below.

Make 8 using dark blue circle fabrics, chartreuse chain fabric, and light blue print circle fabric (2 with each dark blue fabric for scrappy version).

4. Repeat to make 4 Log Cabin blocks using fabrics as shown in the diagram below.

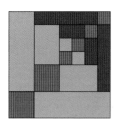

Make 4 using green circle fabrics, light purple chain fabric, and purple outer background fabric (1 with each green fabric for scrappy version).

5. Repeat to make 8 of each of the following 2 Log Cabin blocks using fabric as shown in the diagrams below.

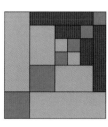

Make 8 using green circle fabrics, medium blue outer chain fabric, and purple outer background fabric (2 with each green fabric for scrappy version).

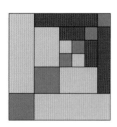

Make 8 using light blue circle fabrics, medium blue outer chain fabric, and purple outer background fabric.

quilt assembly

1. Referring to the quilt assembly diagram for your quilt size, pages 93–94, place all the Log Cabin blocks and the remaining squares and rectangles for the sashing and teal inner border on the design wall. If you are using 4 dark blues and 4 greens for the circles, make sure the blocks using the same fabric are grouped together. The blues will form a complete circle, and the greens will form three-quarters of a circle.

2. Sew the parts together to form each section as shown. Follow the pressing arrows carefully.

3. Sew the sections together to form the center of the quilt top. Press.

4. Referring to Adding Borders, page 18, measure and trim outer border strips. Pin and sew the side borders to the quilt. Press the seams toward the outer borders. Pin and sew the top and bottom borders to the quilt. Press the seams toward the outer borders.

5. Layer, baste, and quilt as desired. Bind and add a label.

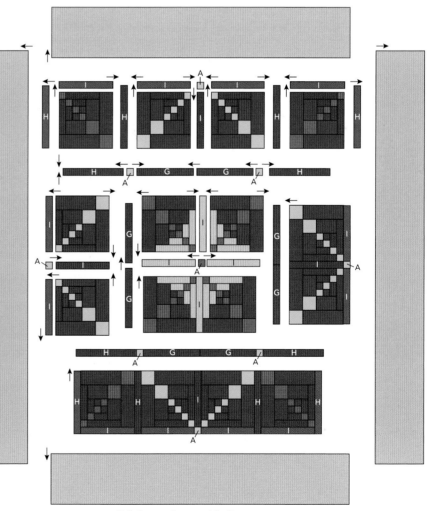

Crib/Lap quilt assembly diagram

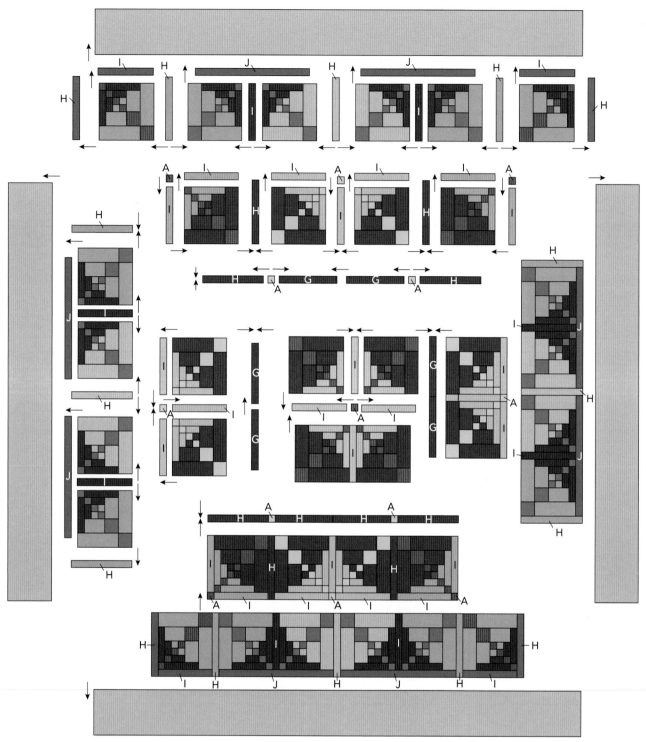

Twin/Double and Queen/King quilt assembly diagram

ABOUT THE AUTHOR

Although she enjoyed her former career as a professional violinist, this phase of Laurie Shifrin's life has been the most creative and rewarding. She feels fortunate to live in the lush Pacific Northwest, where her love for colors and textures found in nature is constantly fed and nurtured.

Laurie has authored two previous books on using batiks, but this is her first with C&T Publishing. Being a published author has opened up the world of international teaching. Laurie regularly travels around the United States and Canada to share her enthusiasm and love for batiks and her no-nonsense quilting tips. Her appearance on the television show *Simply Quilts with Alex Anderson* is still shown in reruns.

Many quilters know Laurie from her many years as manager of the wonderful Seattle quilt shop In The Beginning, which closed its doors a few years ago. She continues as a technical editor for In The Beginning publications, including books and patterns.

Laurie's other quilting endeavors have led her to design the featured pattern for a batik kit from Timeless Treasures. She has contributed quilts to numerous books by other authors, including a recently released book on table runners. Laurie's quilts and quilt designs are regularly featured by Hoffman, Island Batik, and Princess Mirah Design at International Quilt Market.

RESOURCES

For a list of other fine books from C&T Publishing, ask for a free catalog:

C&T Publishing, Inc.
P.O. Box 1456
Lafayette, CA 94549
(800) 284-1114
Email: ctinfo@ctpub.com
Website: www.ctpub.com

C&T Publishing's professional photography services are now available to the public. Visit us at www.ctmediaservices.com.

For quilting supplies:

Cotton Patch
1025 Brown Ave.
Lafayette, CA 94549
(800) 835-4418 or
(925) 283-7883
Email: CottonPa@aol.com
Website: www.quiltusa.com

Batik Fabrics

More than a dozen companies offer batiks. A few of my favorite suppliers are the following:

Bold Over Batiks!
(www.boldoverbatiks.com)

Hoffman California-International Fabrics (www.hoffmanfabrics.com)

Island Batik, Inc.
(www.islandbatik.com)

Princess Mirah Design / Bali Fabrics
(www.balifab.com)

Timeless Treasures
(www.ttfabrics.com)

Note: Fabrics used in the quilts shown may not be currently available, as fabric manufacturers keep most fabrics in print for only a short time.

Cotton Batting

Quilters Dream Batting is available from your local quilt shop or Hancock's of Paducah.

General Quilting Book

Hargrave, Harriet, and Sharyn Craig. *The Art of Classic Quiltmaking.* Lafayette, CA: C&T Publishing, 2000.

Notions

Quilt Wall is available from Keepsake Quilting (www.keepsakequilting)

All other notions mentioned are readily available at most quilt shops.